THE WICCAN'S

BOOK

of

MEDIEVAL

WITCHCRAFT

Spells, Potions and Fortune Telling

SPECIAL THANKS TO:
WILLIAM SALMON
L.W. DE LAURENCE
M. YOUNG
EBENEZER SIBLY
NICHOLAS CULPEPER
JOHN LYDGATE
JOHANN WECKER
HILDEGARD OF BINGEN
CHARLES GODFREY LELAND
AND THE ANONYMOUS ONES.

"IF NEVER TO DO HARM, BE TO DO GOOD, I DARE SAY I AM NOT ILL."

~~ MOTHER BOMBIE

To Make a Holy Salve
which shall preserve against all evil

Take betony and bennet, blue nettle and blueweed,
Sedge and sage, smallage and stitchwort,
Hindheal, horehound, houndstongue and hemp,
Shoots of hellebore, strawberry stalk,
Field balm, fennel, and five-finger grass,
Fleur de lys, feverfew, fennel-flower, flag,
Woodwaxen, woodruff, mugwort and dill,
Periwinkle, pennyroyal, agrimony, alexanders,
English costmary, blessed thistle,
Raspberry, rosemary, red yarrow, rue,
Savory, southernwood, black snail's dust,
Cow parsley, cumin, cockspur and kale,
Water betony, radish leaf,
Juniper, gentian, lupin and lovage,
Wormwood and throatwort, along with verbena,
Black centaury, celandine, parsley and groundsel,
Myrtle bark, tarragon, mollyblobs, meadowsweet.

Beat it in butter from a cow of one color,
And chant nine times over the whole of it,
thus:

ACRE ACRE ARNEM NONA
AERNEM BEOTHOR AERNEM HIDREN
ARCUM CUNATH ELE HARASSAN FIDINE.

The Power of Planets and eke The Stars,
And of every heavenly intelligence,
Disposition of peace and eke of wars,
And of each strange other science
As the seven gods by their influence

))

Whenever you wish to reveal or to hide,
Herbs of the Moon you shall find need be tried.
They also, because of the Moon's variation,
Are useful when looking to vary your station.

Adder's tongue, arrach, chick-weed, clary sage, wild clary, cleavers, cucumber, dog rose, dog's tooth violet, eryngo, faverel, yellow flag, fluellen, garden iris, lady's smock, lettuce, all lilies, loosestrife, french mercury, orpine, poppy, pumpkin,

RATTLE-GRASS, SAXIFRAGE, SOLDIER, STONE-CROP, WALLFLOWER, WILLOW TREE.

♂

THE WORTS OF MARS ARE OFT TIMES USED
WHEN YOU OR ELSE HAVE BEEN ABUSED.
THEY AID YOU IN COURAGE AND STRENGTHEN YOUR MIGHT
AND GIVE YOU SUCCESSES WHEN FORCED TO FIGHT.

ANEMONE, ARSSMART, ASARABACCA, BARBERRY, BASIL, BLESSED THISTLE, BROOK-LIME, BRYONY, BUTCHER'S BROOM, LESSER CELANDINE, CHIVES, CROWFOOT, CUCKOO-PINT, YELLOW DAFFODIL, DOVE'S FOOT, COTTON THISTLE, EVEWEED, FLAXWEED, GALANGAL, GARLIC, GENTIAN, GERMANDER, GOATSTHORN, GROUND PINE, HAWTHORN, HONEYSUCKLE, HOPS, HEDGE HYSSOP, GREAT WILD LETTUCE, LUPIN, MADDER, MASTERWORT, ALL MUSTARDS, ALL NETTLES, ONION, ALL PEPPERS, PINE TREE, COMMON RADISH, HORSERADISH, REST-HARROW, RHUBARB, SALTWORT, SANICLE,

SARSAPARILLA, SAVINE, SHEPHERD'S ROD, BLUE SIMSON, SOWBREAD, SQUILL, SUN SPURGE, TARRAGON, TOBACCO, WOODRUFF, WORMSEED, WORMWOOD.

☿

MERCURY'S HERBS MUST BE AT HAND
WHEN SOMEONE NEEDS SPEAK OR TO MAKE UNDERSTAND,
AND EKE MASTER MERCURY HELPETH IN NEED
FOR ANOTHER GOOD POWER OF HIS IS TO SPEED.

AGARIC, BITTERSWEET, CALAMINT, CARAWAY, CARROT, DILL, DOG'S MERCURY, ELECAMPANE, ALL FENNELS, FENUGREEK, BRAKE FERN, FLAX, GOAT'S RUE, HAZELNUT WOOD OR FRUIT, GOOD HENRY, ALL HOREHOUNDS, HOUNDS-TONGUE, ALL LAVENDERS, LILY OF THE VALLEY, LICORICE, MAIDENHAIR, MAN-DRAKE, ALL MARJORAMS, MULBERRY TREE OR FRUIT, MUSHROOM, MYRTLE TREE, COMMON PARSLEY, ALL PELLITORIES, POMEGRANATE FRUIT OR LEAVES, RAMPION, GARLIC CRESS, ALL SAVORIES, ALL

SCABIOUS', SENNA, SMALLAGE, SOUTHERNWOOD, SPIGNEL, TREFOIL, VALERIAN.

♃

JUPITER'S HERBAGE CAN MAKE YOU MORE SPRY

SHOULD ANYTHING HEALTHWISE FOR YOU GO AWRY,

AND ANY TIME BUSINESS OR LUCK START TO STALE,

THEY BUILD UP YOUR FORTUNES TILL HEARTY AND HALE.

ALL AGRIMONIES, ALEXANDERS, ASPARAGUS, AVENS, BALM, WHITE BEETS, ALL BETONIES, BILBERRIES, BORAGE, CHERVIL, CHESTNUT TREE OR FRUIT, CINQUEFOIL, COSTMARY, DANDELION, DOCK, DOG GRASS, EGLANTINE, ENDIVE, FIG FRUIT OR LEAVES, FIR, GOATSBEARD, HIND'S TONGUE, HOUSE-LEEK, HYSSOP, JASMINE OR JESSAMINE, LANG DE BOEUF, DOG LICHEN, LIME TREE, LUNGWORT, MAPLE TREE, MEADOWSWEET, OAK TREE, POLYPODY, SAGE, SAMPHIRE, SCURVY GRASS, SUCCORY, SUMACH, SWALLOW-WORT, THORN-APPLE.

♀

Venus' herbs are put to prove
For tasks of beauty and of love.
Another thing Dame Venus brings
Are shining riches, as for kings.

all ALDERS, ALEHOOF, ALKANET, ARCHANGEL, BROAD BEANS, FRENCH BEANS, BIRCH, BLACKBERRY, BUGLE, BURDOCK, CATNIP, CHERRIES or BARK OF CHERRY, COLTSFOOT, COLUMBINE, COWSLIP, CUDWEED, DAFFOLDIL, all DAISIES, DITTANDER, all DITTANIES, DROPWORT, all ELDERS, FEVERFEW, FIG-WORT, all FLEABANES, FOXGLOVE, GOLDENROD, GOOSEBERRY, GROUNDSEL, HERB ROBERT, HERB TRUE-LOVE, HOLLYHOCKS, KIDNEYWORT, LADY'S BEDSTRAW, LADY'S MANTLE, LENTILS, all MALLOWS, MAYWEED, all MINTS, MONEYWORT, MOTHERWORT, MUGWORT, ORACH, ORCHID, PEACH TREE or FRUIT, PEAR TREE or FRUIT, PENNYROYAL, PENNYWORT, PERIWINKLE, PLANTAIN, PLOUGHMAN'S SPIKENARD, PLUM TREE or FRUIT, BUCK'S HORN,

PRIMROSE, RAGWORT, RASPBERRY, ROCKET
CRESS, ROSE, WOOD SAGE, SELF-HEAL,
SILVERWEED, SKIRRET, SOAPWORT, ALL SORRELS,
SOW THISTLE, STRAWBERRIES, SYCAMORE TREE,
TANSY, TEASEL, THYME AND WILD THYME,
VERVAIN, VIOLET, WHEAT, YARROW.

♄

WHEN SOMETHING SEEMS BEYOND YOUR GRASP
YET YOU WOULD HAVE IT IN YOUR CLASP
TURN YOU TO SATURNLY HERB, ROOT OR FLOWER.
THEY SHALL PROVIDE YOU THE REQUISITE POWER.

ACONITE, AMARANTHUS, ARSSMART, BARLEY,
RED BEETS, BISTORT, BLUE-BOTTLE, BUCKTHORN,
CLOWN'S WOUNDWORT, COMFREY, CROSSWORT,
DARNEL, DODDER OF THYME, ELM, ROYAL FERN,
FLUXWEED, FUMITORY, GALL-OAK, GLADIOLE,
GLAWIN, GOUT-WEED, WINTERGREEN,
HAWKWEED, HEARTSEASE, ALL HELLEBORES,
HEMLOCK, HEMP, HENBANE, HERB
CHRISTOPHER, HOLLY, HORSETAIL, IVY,
KNAPWEED, KNAPWORT, KNOTGRASS,

MEZEREON SPURGE, ALL MULLEINS, ALL NIGHTSHADES, ALL POPLARS, QUINCE TREE OR FRUIT, ROOT OF SCARCITY, MEADOW SAFFRON, SAFFLOWER, SHEPHERD'S PURSE, SLOE BUSH, SOLOMON'S SEAL, WATER VIOLET, ALL WILLOWHERBS.

⊙

YOU WISH FOR THIS, YOU WISH FOR THAT,

BUT *OMNIA SOL TEMPERAT*,

AND SO THE SUN DOTH RULE IT ALL

WHEN ANY GOODLY NEED BEFALL.

ANGELICA, ASH TREE, BAY, BURNET, BUTTER-BUR, GREATER CELANDINE, CENTAURY, CHAMOMILE, EYEBRIGHT, CORN FEVERFEW, JUNIPER TREE, LOVAGE, MISTLETOE, PEONY, RICE, ROSEMARY, RUE, SAFFRON, ST. JOHN'S WORT, STORAX TREE, SUNDEW, TORMENTIL, GRAPE VINE OR GRAPES, VIPER'S BUGLOSS, WALNUT TREE OR FRUIT, YEW TREE.

On the Gathering of Herbs

Such barks, fruits, leaves and so on as do face the rising sun are the most potent and powerful. These herbs you shall gather by night, before the sun should rise. Be you barefoot, and be you silent throughout the whole procedure. You shall gather the herbs, barks and roots, but use not any iron utensil as you do so. Above the plants which you have gathered, you will speak as written here: O God, who at the beginning of the world commanded the verdant plants to grow and multiply, we offer humble and suppliant prayers that you may bless and consecrate in your name these herbs, gathered for helpful use, so that all who make use of them may deserve to obtain peace in mind and body.

You shall carry the herbs with you, or strew them about your house, to affect their purpose; or else you may form them into unguents or potions, which must always be

MADE FROM SEVEN HERBS, OR NINE. AND ROSE MAY MAKE ANY POTION OR UNGUENT SO MUCH THE BETTER FOR ALL OF ITS GOOD VIRTUES, EVEN IF JUST A LITTLE IS ADDED THERETO.

EXCEEDING THE GENERAL USAGE THAT HATH BEEN AFORESAID, YOU MAY AVAIL YOURSELF OF THE FOLLOWING WORKINGS IN PARTICULAR:

I. CARRY WITH YOU WORMWOOD SO AS TO WARD AWAY ALL SORCERIES.

II. BIND SPRIGS OF ROSEMARY ABOUT YOUR DOOR TO WARD AWAY SNAKES, OR CARRY THE SPRIGS TO KEEP AWAY EVIL SPIRITS AND ELVES.

III. FIVE LEAVES OF THE NETTLE, CARRIED, ENSURE AGAINST FEAR OR FANTASY.

IV. TO CARRY MISTLETOE ENSURES ONE WINS IN COURT OR LEGAL MATTERS.

V. IF YOU ARE TROUBLED BY A WICKED PERSON WHO LEADS YOU TO BAD BEHAVIORS AND THOUGHTS, RUB HIM WITH THE ROOT OF CELERY AND A GREAT CHANGE SHALL BE EFFECTED.

VI. TO CAUSE IMPOTENCE, YOU SHALL EAT THE FLOWERS OF WILLOW OR POPLAR.

VII. Fumitory, burnt, shall release a smoke which dispelleth all evil spirits.

VIII. To judge the severity of any man's illness, hold vervain to the head of the sick one, and ask him how he feels. He will be unable to answer falsely.

IX. One who carries periwinkle shall be prosperous and ever acceptable, and it guards against witlessness or demoniacal possession, and against snakes and wild beasts.

X. And if you would be cheerful and have a good memory, eat nightly of balm.

The Making of Potions

You shall take your herbs, spices, gums or what else have you, and grind them up small in a mortar. And then you shall cast them in a bottle or another vessel which may be stopped, and pour upon them aqua vitae, as much as you need to cover the said herbs; and if you cannot have aqua vitae, you shall use wine or sack. And you shall leave these together for some days to digest, stopped up in the bottle, and you may shake it by and by. When enough time has passed, you shall strain the aqua vitae through a cloth, and if there are any herbs left you shall cast them in a river. And to the aqua vitae you shall cast there oil of palma Christi, and stir it, and keep it for your use.

The Making of Unguents

You shall take any solid grease or fat, of whatever sort is best for your use. You shall

HAVE YOUR POWDERS OR YOUR HERBS STILL FRESH, AND SEETHE THEM IN THE GREASE ALONG WITH WINE OR SACK, AND WHEN THE WINE HATH BOILED AWAY YOU MAY POUR IT THROUGH A STRAINER OR A CLOTH IF IT IS NOT YET TOO HOT, AND YOU SHALL DO AWAY WITH THE HERBS IN A RIVER, AND YOU SHALL KEEP THE GREASE FOR YOUR USE. AND IF YOU WOULD MAKE IT BETTER, YOU MAY ADD THERETO ROSEWATER AND LIQUID GREASE (AS OIL OF BEN OR PALMA CHRISTI) AND BEAT THEM WELL TOGETHER.

Hungary Water
For beauty

Take fresh rosemary tops and weigh out four times as much of aqua vitae, and leave this to soak for half a day, and then you shall draw it in a bain marie till the liquid be but small. And this is the water of Saint Elizabeth of Hungary, which shall be used.

To Write On Paper a Letter
Which none shall see until the paper is heated

Take sal ammoniac and soak it in water till it dissolves, then write with this as your ink, and let it dry, and it will last about eight days.

To Make Rosewater
Without an Alembic

Take two bowls of glass, and tuck a kerchief across the top of one in the manner of a drum, and spread your fresh roses upon it. Lay the other bowl upon it, and set this all out in the sun, and the heat of the sun will cause the rosewater to form.

To Calm All Bitterness
of the Heart and Mind

To sharpen the senses and diminish all harmful humors of the body, take some nutmeg and an equal weight of cinnamon, and a few cloves, and grind them to a powder. Make them into small cakes along with fine wheat flour and water, and eat these frequently.

To Lessen Wrath and be Made Happy

A man that inclineth to wrath shall take rose and a lesser amount of sage, and powder them together, and he shall hold this powder to his nose whenever wrath is rising.

Borage Wine
Good for melancholy people, and pains of the heart, making men merry and curing madness, et cetera.

Take borage flowers, as many as you please; put them into new wine until it be fully saturated, and when it is settled, pour it off into another vessel gently, and keep it for your use.

Of the Matter

of which

Perfumes are Made

I. The ground of vegetable perfumes, is taken from flowers, seeds, herbs, roots, woods, and gums.

II. The chief flowers for this use, are of clove-gillyflowers, roses, jasmine, lavender, oranges and saffron.

III. The chief seeds or fruits are nutmegs, cloves; caraways, grains of paradise, seeds of geranium moschatum, the nut ben.

IV. The chief herbs are geranium moschatum, basil, sweet marjoram, thyme, angelica, rosemary, lavender, hyssop, sweet trefoil, mint and bay-tree leaves.

V. The chief roots are calamus aromaticus, ginger, galangal, caryophyllata, Indian spikenard and sweet orris or iris.

VI. The chief woods are of yellow sandalwood, balsamum, lignum aloes, and rhodium.

VII. The barks and peels are of cinnamon, oranges, lemons and citrons.

VIII. The chief gums are frankincense, olibanum, labdanum, styrax, liquid styrax, balsamum verum, ambergris, styrax calamita, benzoin, amber, camphor.

IX. The chief matters of perfumes taken from animals, are musk, civet, cow-dung and other turds.

X. Of minerals there are two only, which yield a perfume, and they are antimony and sulfur.

The way to extract perfuming essences is somewhat difficult, that is to say, by distillation calcination, digestion or by menstruum. However, to make a perfume of oil is very simple. You shall put your musk, amber, etc. in fine powder to your oil, the which, keep in a glass bottle very close

STOPPED, FOR A MONTH OR MORE, AND THEN USE IT. THE BEST OIL TO USE FOR THIS PURPOSE IS THAT WHICH IS CALLED BEN; THIS OIL OF BEN HATH TWO PROPERTIES, THE ONE IS, THAT HAVING NO SCENT OR ODOR OF ITSELF, IT ALTERS, CHANGES OR DIMINISHES NOT THE SCENT OF ANY PERFUME PUT INTO IT: THE OTHER IS THAT IT IS OF A LONG CONTINUANCE, SO THAT IT SCARCELY EVER CHANGETH, GROWS RANK, CORRUPTS OR PUTREFIES, AS OTHER OILS DO.

IT HATH ALSO BEEN SAID THAT ONE MAY FASHION PERFUMING INCENSE FOR EACH OF THE PLANETS AS FOLLOWS: ANY FLOWERS MIXED FOR VENUS, ANY FRUITS OR SEEDS MIXED FOR JUPITER, ANY HERBS MIXED FOR THE MOON, ANY ROOTS MIXED FOR SATURN, ANY WOODS MIXED FOR MARS, AND ANY PEELS OR BARKS MIXED FOR MERCURY, AND ANY GUMS MIXED FOR THE SUN. AND THESE ARE BURNT UPON A COAL OR A HOT PLATE OR A HOT SHOVEL.

Of Perfuming Powders

To Make Powder of Ox Dung. Take red ox dung in the month of May and dry it well, make it into an impalpable powder by grinding: it is an excellent perfume without any other addition, yet if you add to one pound of the former, musk, and ambergris of each one dram, it will be beyond comparison.

To Make Cyprian Powder. Gather musk moss of the oak in December, January or February, wash it very clean in rosewater, then dry it, steep it in rosewater for two days, then dry it again, which do oftentimes, and then bring it into fine powder and burn it; of which take one pound, musk one ounce, ambergris half an ounce, civet two drams, yellow sandalwood in powder two ounces, mix all well together in a marble mortar.

Another Way to Make the Same. Take of the aforesaid powder of oak-moss one pound, benzoin, storax, of each two ounces, in fine powder; musk, ambergris and civet of each three drams, mix them well in a mortar.

A Sweet Powder to Lay Among Clothes. Take Damask-rose leaves dried one pound, musk half a dram, violet leaves three ounces, mix them.

Another for the Same or to Wear About One. Take rose leaves dried one pound, cloves in powder half an ounce, spikenard two drams, storax, cinnamon of each three drams, musk half a dram, mix them and put them into bags for use.

Powder of Sweet Orris, the First Way. Take Florentine orris root in powder one pound, benzoin, cloves of each four ounces in powder, mix them.

Powder of Florentine Orris, the Second Way. Take of orris root six ounces, rose leaves in powder four ounces, marjoram, cloves, storax in powder of each one ounce, benzoin, yellow sandalwood of each half an ounce, violets four ounces, musk one dram, cypress half a dram. Mix them: being grossly powdered, put them into bags to lay amongst linen: but being fine, they will serve for other uses; as we shall show.

POWDER OF ORRIS ROOTS, THE THIRD WAY, EXCELLENT FOR LINEN IN BAGS. TAKE ROOTS OF IRIS ONE POUND, SWEET MARJORAM TWELVE OUNCES, FLOWERS OF ROSEMARY AND ROMAN CHAMOMILE, LEAVES OF THYME, GERANIUM MOSCHATUM, SAVORY EACH FOUR OUNCES, CYPRESS ROOTS, BENZOIN, YELLOW SANDALWOOD, LIGNUM RHODIUM, CITRON PEEL, STORAX, LABDANUM, CLOVES, CINNAMON OF EACH ONE OUNCES, MUSK TWO DRAMS, CIVET ONE DRAM AND A HALF, AMBERGRIS ONE DRAM, POWDER AND MIX THEM FOR BAGS. THIS COMPOSITION WILL RETAIN ITS STRENGTH NEAR TWENTY YEARS.

POWDER OF ORRIS, THE FOURTH WAY. TAKE ORRIS ROOTS IN POWDER ONE POUND, CALAMUS AROMATICUS, CLOVES, DRIED ROSE LEAVES, CORIANDER SEED, GERANIUM MOSCHATUM OF EACH THREE OUNCES, LIGNUM ALOES, MARJORAM, ORANGE PEELS OF EACH ONE OUNCE, STORAX ONE OUNCE AND A HALF, LABDANUM HALF AN OUNCE, LAVENDER, SPIKENARD OF EACH FOUR OUNCES, POWDER ALL AND MIX THEM, TO WHICH ADD MUSK, AMBERGRIS OF EACH TWO SCRUPLES.

Composite Powder of Calamus Aromaticus. Take calamus aromaticus, yellow sandalwood of each one ounce, marjoram, geranium moschatum of each one ounce, rose leaves, violets, of each two drams, nutmegs, cloves of each one dram, musk half a dram, make all into powder, which put in bags for linen.

Another of the Same. Take calamus aromaticus, Florentine iris roots of each two ounces, violet flowers dried one ounce, round cypress roots two drams, adeps rosarum one dram and a half, reduce all into a very fine powder: it is excellent to lay among linen, or to strew in the hair.

An Excellent Perfuming Powder for the Hair. Take Iris roots in fine powder one ounce and a half, benzoin, storax, cloves, musk of each two drams: being all in fine powder, mix them for a perfume for hair powder. Take of this perfume one dram, rice flower impalpable one pound, mix them for a powder for the hair. Note, some use white starch, flower of French beans and the like.

A Sweet Powder for a Silk Bag. Take benzoin, storax calamita, cloves, lignum aloes, of each two ounces, yellow sandalwood three ounces, Florentine orris six ounces, musk half a dram, mingle them.

Another for the Same. Take Florentine orris, spikenard, sweet marjoram dried, geranium moschatum of each four ounces, Damask roses, cypress, lavender flowers, of each three ounces, benzoin, lignum rhodium, of each an ounce, mix them.

Another for the Like Intention. Take Damask roses, yellow sandalwood, lignum aloes, of each four ounces, benzoin, spikenard, cypress, of each two ounces, mingle them together.

Another for the Same Purpose. Take Damask rose leaves a handful, cut off the whites, put them in a glass, and put to them musk half a scruple, ambergris six grains, civet four grains, stop the glass close, and set it in the sun till the leaves be thoroughly dry.

A Powder for a Sweet Bag. Take orris, cypress, white sandalwood, lavender, Damask roses, of each four ounces, calamus, storax

CALAMITA, BENZOIN, SWEET BASIL, SWEET MARJORAM, GERANIUM MOSCHATUM, OF EACH TWO OUNCES, CLOVES, ROSEMARY FLOWERS, OF EACH ONE OUNCE, MIX THEM.

ANOTHER SWEET BAG. TAKE DAMASK ROSES FOUR OUNCES AND A HALF; MARJORAM, ORRIS, OF EACH FOUR OUNCES, GERANIUM MOSCHATUM THREE OUNCES, LABDANUM TWO OUNCES AND A HALF, LIGNUM ALOES, WHITE SANDALWOOD, CLOVES, CYPRESS, BENZOIN, CALAMUS, OF EACH TWO OUNCES, MUSK, AMBERGRIS, OF EACH ONE DRAM, MINGLE THEM.

WHITE DAMASK POWDER. TAKE ORRIS IN POWDER, WHITE STARCH, OF EACH EIGHT OUNCES, FINE MUSK A SCRUPLE, MIX IT FIRST WITH A LITTLE, THEN WITH MORE, AND LASTLY WITH THE WHOLE BY DEGREES, THE LONGER IT IS KEPT THE BETTER

ANOTHER DAMASK POWDER. TAKE DAMASK ROSES IN POWDER TWO OUNCES AND A HALF; CALAMUS, ORRIS, CYPRESS, GERANIUM MOSCHATUM, LAVENDER FLOWERS, SWEET MARJORAM, LABDANUM, OF EACH TWO OUNCES, BENZOIN, STORAX CALAMITA, OF EACH AN OUNCE AND HALF; NIGELLA ROMANA ONE

OUNCE; MUSK, AMBERGRIS, OF EACH A DRAM, MINGLE THEM.

ANOTHER DAMASK POWDER. TAKE ORRIS FOUR OUNCES; CLOVES TWO OUNCES; LABDANUM, CYPRESS, BENZOIN, OF EACH ONE OUNCE; CALAMUS, STORAX CALAMITA, OF EACH HALF AN OUNCE; CIVET, MUSK, OF EACH TEN GRAINS, MIX THEM.

ANOTHER SWEET POWDER. TAKE ORRIS SIX OUNCES, CLOVES FOUR OUNCES; YELLOW SANDALWOOD, STORAX CALAMITA, ANA, TWO OUNCES, LABDANUM ONE OUNCE, MUSK A SCRUPLE, MAKE A POWDER.

To Make the Witches Ointment

To make the famous ointment, that you may seem to travel and enjoy great pleasures: in oil combine water parsley, acorns, cinquefoil, blood of a bat, and the sleepy nightshade, and let this seethe with a little water thereto. When it is ready, you shall rub your parts till they be red and the blood warmed near the surface, then apply the ointment thereupon, and this must be done in the dark of night with no fires or lamps lit nearby. And all the day before feed only upon beets, roots and chestnuts, that your visions will be merry.

To Make a Holy Incense

Take unto you sweet spices, stacte, and onycha, and galbanum; these sweet spices with pure frankincense, of each shall there be a like weight, and you shall powder them together.

The Four Things of
Good Fortune

To prepare this charm, you shall take a little red bag, the which must be composed from woolen and of coarse cloth, and you shall sew it with red woolen thread, but not with any silk or cotton; and while sewing it, sing:

I sew this bag for luck to me,
and also for my family;
that it may keep, by night or day,
grief and ailments far away.

Then take a crumb of bread, and a little coarse salt, a sprig of rue, and some cumin, and keep repeating, while making it up, the same chant. And when made, the charm must always be borne on the same person, by night as well as by day.

To Make the Witch's Bottle
Which shall cure of all sorceries
done against ye

You must have a bottle which sealeth with a cork or wooden plug, in which you shall place the following:

A quart of your own piss shall be taken and boiled with a paring from each toenail, and with some of your hair, for fire will burn away all evils, and as the water reduces so shall your trouble. Put thereto sulfur, XII nails made from iron, and VIII pins of brass. Add also a heart that has been shaped and cut from leather or cloth, which you shall pierce with one more nail or pin, for that is the heart of the evil doer who must now be undone and have his ill work returned unto him.

ALL THIS TO THE BOTTLE GOES, WHERE IT IS STOPPED UP, AND SHALL BE BURIED OUTSIDE YOUR HOME, OR IF YOU ARE IN THE CITY, YOU MAY TUCK IT WITHIN YOUR CHIMNEY, AND FOR AS LONG AS THIS REMAINS UNMOLESTED YOU SHALL BE WELL.

Dreams & Visions
THEIR INTERPRETATION AND MEANING

DREAMS ARE INFUSED OR OTHERWISE OCCASIONED IN THE SOUL OF MAN FOR HIS INSTRUCTION AND WARNING. THE INTERPRETATION OF DREAMS CAN FURNISH REVELATIONS OF OUR DESTINY, LIKE SOME OTHER OCCULT SCIENCES. AS REGARDS THE INTERPRETATION ITSELF, THERE ARE NEITHER GENERAL NOR PARTICULAR LAWS, BUT THERE IS A VERY LARGE BODY OF MEANINGS OR EXPLAINED CASES WHICH COVER MOST OF THE EXPERIENCES OBTAINED IN SLEEP; AND THESE MEANINGS ARE A RESULT OF ANCIENT OBSERVATION WHICH HAS COME DOWN TO OUR DAYS. THE ANCIENTS SAY THAT WHEN THE BODY IS ASLEEP THE SPIRIT MAINTAINS ITS VIGIL, PROCEEDS AT WILL WHERESOEVER THE BODY CAN GO, AND BEHOLDS ALL THAT THE PHYSICAL EYES CAN DISCERN IN THE WAKING STATE. CERTAIN GIFTED SOULS CAN TRANSCEND THE NORMAL SPHERE OF VISION AND ENTER INTO HIDDEN WORLDS.

There are four kinds of dream, to which different names are given, according to the quality of each: the first is simple dream, the second vision, the third reverie, while the fourth is called apparition.

I. In simple dream the truth is held to be manifested under certain symbolic images; it is a kind of picture-writing or pageant enacted within the psychic nature of the dreaming man, but sometimes in such a manner that he is actor-in-chief. As an instance of the simplest kind, Pharaoh beheld a group of seven fat kine and then another group consisting of seven lean beasts, but it was Joseph who gave him the meaning. Septimus Severus succeeded Pertinax after dreaming that he had taken possession of the horse which threw the emperor mentioned. Queen Hecuba, with child of the notorious Paris, brought forth in a dream a firebrand which consumed the city of Troy. Astyage, King of Medea, saw his daughter give birth to a vinestalk, and in due course he

BECAME THE GRANDFATHER OF ILLUSTRIOUS CYRUS. THE QUEEN OF MACEDONIA DREAMED THAT SHE WAS STAMPED ON THE BREAST WITH A SEAL REPRESENTING A LION, AND THIS TOOK PLACE WHEN SHE WAS BEARING THE GREAT ALEXANDER WITHIN HER. AMILCAR WAS WARNED IN HIS SLEEP THAT HE WOULD SUP ON THE MORROW IN A BELEAGUERED CITY, AND HE ENTERED ONE AS A FACT, BUT IT WAS IN THE GUISE OF A PRISONER OF WAR. DREAMS OF THIS KIND ARE ENDLESS.

II. THE USUAL CHARACTERISTIC OF VISION IS THAT IT TAKES PLACE IN THE WAKING STATE, AND AT ITS HIGHEST IT MAY BE THAT WHICH IS UNDERSTOOD AS SPIRITUAL REVELATION. A SIMPLE INSTANCE, APART FROM ANY MESSAGE, IS WHEN JACOB WAS MET BY THE ANGELS (SPIRITS) AT THE PLACE WHICH HE CALLED MAHANAIM. THERE ARE ALSO VISIONS OF THE NIGHT WHICH ARE DISTINGUISHED BY THEIR IMPORTANCE FROM DREAMS, BUT THE DISTINCTION IS SOMEWHAT ARBITRARY. THE THREE MAGI WERE WARNED IN THIS MANNER NOT TO RETURN TO HEROD; THE ANGEL (SPIRIT) COMMANDED JOSEPH TO TAKE THE YOUNG CHILD AND HIS MOTHER AND

FLEE INTO EGYPT; THE LADDER WHICH WAS SHOWN IN HIS SLEEP TO JACOB IS CLASSED AS A VISION RATHER THAN A DREAM. ON THE OTHER HAND, PROPHETIC EXPERIENCES LIKE THOSE OF ISAIAH REPRESENT VISION IN THE ABSOLUTE SENSE OF THE WORD AND ARE APART FROM EXPERIENCES IN SLUMBER, WHETHER THESE ARE GREAT OR SMALL.

III. REVERIE, AS IT IS COMMONLY UNDERSTOOD, IS SYNONYMOUS WITH THE STATE OF BROWN STUDY, OR INTENSE PREOCCUPATION; AS SUCH, IT IS WITHOUT CONSEQUENCE AND CALLS FOR NO INTERPRETATION. THERE IS, HOWEVER, AN ARBITRARY USE OF THE TERM WHICH IS FOUND IN A FEW WORKS ON THE INTERPRETATION OF DREAMS; IT IS CONCERNED WITH THE REPETITION IN SLEEP OF STRONG IMPRESSIONS PRESENT TO THE MIND DURING THE WAKING HOURS. THAT WHICH HAS BEEN THOUGHT, AND DEEPLY IN MOST CASES, IN THE DAY IS DREAMED DURING THE NIGHT. PERSONS WHO ARE AFRAID OF CERTAIN UNWELCOME ENCOUNTERS ARE APT TO DREAM THAT THEY HAVE ACTUALLY OCCURRED. SO ALSO HE WHO IS ALWAYS BROODING OVER MONEY WILL HAVE IT WITH HIM IN HIS SLEEP,

AND A SUBSTANTIAL SUPPER IN THE EVENING MAY
REAPPEAR AS A BANQUET AT NIGHT.

IV. THE USE OF THE TERM APPARITION TO
DISTINGUISH A FOURTH ASPECT OF DREAMING SEEMS
TO IDENTIFY THE STATE WITH THAT OF
HALLUCINATION, BECAUSE SUCH APPARITIONS ARE
SAID TO BE SEEN BY THOSE WHO ARE DECREPIT AND
WEAK IN MIND, OR ELSE BY YOUNG CHILDREN.
VERIDIC APPARITIONS WOULD BELONG TO THE
ORDER OF VISIONS. THE READER WILL BE LIKELY TO
DISPOSE RATHER SUMMARILY OF A TABULATION
WHICH WILL HAVE LITTLE TO HIS PURPOSE, AND HE
WILL BE SATISFIED TO REGARD DREAMS AS THINGS
HEARD, SEEN AND ACTED IN SLEEP, WHILE VISIONS,
AS INTIMATED ALREADY, ARE EXPERIENCES IN THE
VIGIL OF WAKING LIFE.

IN RESPECT OF DREAMS, IT HAS BEEN LAID DOWN BY
INTERPRETERS THAT THOSE WHICH ARE ONLY
REMEMBERED IN PART ARE USELESS FOR
EXPLANATORY PURPOSES; THAT THOSE WHICH
OCCUR IMMEDIATELY AFTER RETIREMENT ARE NOT
TO BE TRUSTED, BECAUSE THE PROCESS OF DIGESTION

IS STILL AT WORK IN THE ORGANISM; AND THAT THOSE WHICH BELONG TO THE BREAK OF DAY ARE THOSE WHICH MAY ENTER INTO THE REALM OF SEERSHIP.

THERE ARE FURTHER TWO CHIEF KINDS OF DREAMS, AS DREAMS ARE UNDERSTOOD BY THE CLASSIFICATION ALREADY MADE. THE FIRST KIND IS CALLED SPECULATIVE OR CONTEMPLATIVE. A CASE IN POINT IS THAT OF THE PRISONER WHO DREAMT THAT HE WAS ABOUT TO BE HANGED AND THAT THE ROPE WAS ALREADY ROUND HIS NECK, WHEN ONE WHO STOOD NEAR DREW HIS SWORD AND SET HIM FREE. THIS WAS REALIZED NEXT DAY, FOR HE WAS CONDEMNED TO DEATH AND WAS ALREADY IN THE EXECUTIONER'S HANDS, BUT WAS RESCUED BY ARMED MEN EMPLOYED BY HIS FRIENDS FOR THE PURPOSE. THE SECOND KIND IS CALLED ALLEGORICAL OR SPECULATIVE, AND THEIR FULFILLMENT IS NEVER OF THE LITERAL AND ACTUAL CLASS. THE COMMUNICATION IS BY WAY OF ENIGMA AND SYMBOL. TO SEE A SERPENT IN DREAM PORTENDS ENEMIES AND INGRATITUDE; AN APPEARANCE LIKE THAT OF AN ANGEL (A SPIRIT) IS UNDERSTOOD TO

MEAN REVELATION. THAT WHICH IS SIGNIFIED DOES NOT AS A RULE COME TO PASS FOR AT LEAST SEVERAL DAYS. IT IS TO BE REMARKED THAT ONLY PERSONS OF PURE LIFE, TEMPERATE HABIT, CLEAR UNDERSTANDING, CLAIRVOYANT SIGHT, AND SOUND JUDGMENT ARE LIKELY TO HAVE IMPORTANT DREAMS; EXCESSES, IN EATING AND DRINKING ESPECIALLY, TEND TO CLOUD THE BOND OF KINSHIP WHICH SUBSISTS BETWEEN THE PRESENT AND FUTURE. THE DREAMER'S PHYSICAL AND OTHER CONDITIONS MUST THEREFORE BE KNOWN OR MUST BE GAUGED APPROXIMATELY, BEFORE HIS EXPERIENCES IN SLEEP CAN BE TRANSLATED FOR HIS OWN OR FOR OUR INSTRUCTION.

THEREFORE, HE WHO WOULD RECEIVE TRUE ORACLES BY DREAMS, LET HIM ABSTAIN FROM SUPPER, DRINK, AND BE OTHERWISE WELL DISPOSED, SO THAT HIS BRAIN WILL BE FREE FROM TURBULENT VAPORS. LET HIM HAVE HIS BED-CHAMBER PURE AND CLEAN, LET HIM PERFUME THE SAME WITH SOME FUMIGATION, AND ANOINT HIS TEMPLES WITH SOME UNGUENT EFFACIOUS HEREUNTO, USING HERBS OF THE MOON AS DESCRIBED ELSEWHERE WITHIN THIS TOME.

TABLE OF THE DAYS
OF THE MOON FOR THE INTERPRETATION OF
DREAMS AND VISIONS

THE FIRST DAY OF THE MOON IS THAT OF THE NEW MOON, WHEN THE MOON IS NEW IN THE MORNING. BUT WHEN THE NEW MOON ARRIVES IN ONE OF THE EVENING HOURS, THE FIRST DAY IS COUNTED FROM THE MORNING AFTER. THE LUNAR MONTH HAS SOMETIMES XXIX DAYS AND SOMETIMES XXX, INCLUDING, OF COURSE, THAT PERIOD DURING WHICH IT ABIDES IN THE HIDDENNESS.

FIRST DAY OF THE MOON. DREAMS ARE FORTUNATE.

SECOND DAY. THAT WHICH YOU HAVE DREAMED HAS NO TRUTH IN IT.

THIRD DAY. DREAM IS WITHOUT CONSEQUENCE.

FOURTH DAY. DREAMS ARE FORTUNATE, AND YOU MAY LOOK FOR THEIR FULFILLMENT.

FIFTH DAY. They are entirely futile, and nothing can follow therefrom.

SIXTH DAY. Be very careful, and see that you tell your dream to nobody.

SEVENTH DAY. Keep your dream in mind, because there is truth in it.

EIGHTH DAY. Something will follow from your dreaming. It has a purpose.

NINTH DAY. You will see a result at once.

TENTH DAY. It will be true and will come to pass with joy.

ELEVENTH DAY. The realization will be with you in four days.

TWELFTH DAY. You will have cause to remember your dream, because it will be realized by its opposite.

THIRTEENTH DAY. That which you dream will be true, and there is no question concerning it.

FOURTEENTH DAY. It will happen, but long after.

FIFTEENTH DAY. The realization will be with you in thirty days.

SIXTEENTH DAY. THAT WHICH YOU HAVE DREAMED WILL COME TO PASS.

SEVENTEENTH DAY. TELL NO ONE TILL THE THIRD DAY THEREAFTER.

EIGHTEENTH DAY. BE CAREFUL; THE DREAM IS LIKELY TO BE MADE VOID.

NINETEENTH DAY. KEEP IT IN YOUR MIND. YOU WILL HAVE JOY IN THE HEART BECAUSE OF IT.

TWENTIETH DAY. YOU WILL ASSUREDLY SEE THE RESULT; AND THAT IN FOUR DAYS' TIME.

TWENTY-FIRST DAY. PUT NO TRUST THEREIN, FOR NOTHING WILL COME OF IT.

TWENTY-SECOND DAY. BE PATIENT FOR A FEW DAYS ONLY, AND YOU SHALL SEE WHAT YOU SHALL SEE.

TWENTY-THIRD DAY. THE DREAM WILL BE FULFILLED IN THREE DAYS.

TWENTY-FOURTH DAY. IT WILL BRING YOU MUCH SATISFACTION.

TWENTY-FIFTH DAY. IT WILL COME TO PASS IN EIGHT OR NINE DAYS.

TWENTY-SIXTH DAY. TAKE HEED. THIS IS IMPORTANT FOR YOU.

TWENTY-SEVENTH DAY. GREAT CONTENTMENT
WILL FOLLOW HEREON.

TWENTY-EIGHTH DAY. IT IS TRUE AND WILL COME
TO PASS WITH JOY.

TWENTY-NINTH DAY. REST ASSURED THE DREAM
IS TRUE.

THIRTIETH DAY. IT WILL COME TO PASS ON THE
SAME MORNING.

SYMBOLISM OF
THE FOUR ELEMENTS
IN THE WORLD OF DREAM

THE PRESAGES OF FIRE

I. THOSE WHO ARE ACCUSTOMED TO SEE FIRE IN THEIR SLEEP ARE PROMPT AND CHOLERIC IN THEIR TEMPERAMENT. THE DREAM OF FIRE IS USUALLY AN AFTERMATH OF ANGER, TO WHICH THE PERSON SO TROUBLED HAS BEEN SUBJECT THE DAY PREVIOUSLY.

II. TO BE SCORCHED IN DREAM SIGNIFIES AN ATTACK OF SLIGHT FEVER.

III. TO SEE A SLOW FIRE, WITHOUT SPARKS OR SMOKE, ARGUES PERFECT HEALTH; SOMETIMES AN ABUNDANCE OF GOOD THINGS; AND SOMETIMES A FEAST OR OTHER REJOICING IN THE COMPANY OF RELATIVES AND FRIENDS.

IV. A GREAT FIRE, FULL OF SPARKS AND SMOKE, FORETELLS UNWELCOME NEWS OR QUARRELS OF A MINOR KIND.

V. TO SEE FIRE EXTINGUISHED MEANS POVERTY, WANT, BAD FORTUNE; BUT IN THE CASE OF A SICK PERSON, IT MEANS SPEEDY CURE.

VI. A lighted candle or lantern, burning brightly, promises restoration to health, supposing that the dreamer is ill. It is also a sign of marriage for single persons, and generally of success in undertakings.

VII. A lantern or candle burning in a dull manner, or extinguished, forebodes sadness or sickness, but neither will last long.

VIII. To dream that one is in a ship and watching a far-off light burning clearly means that no wind will trouble us and that we shall come into port safely. This may refer to enterprises as well as voyaging.

IX. It is a good sign to dream that one is holding a lighted torch. In the case of young people, they will be fortunate in love, will attain their end, overcome their enemies and be honored and welcomed by everyone.

X. To dream that another person is holding a lighted torch signifies that the evil which we have done will be discovered and that requital will follow.

XI. An extinguished torch has the opposite meaning in each of the above cases.

XII. To see a house burning with a clear, silent, unconsuming fire means possessions for those who are destitute, riches and inheritance. Those who are rich already will have honors conferred upon them, whether in the way of charges, dignities, or otherwise.

XIII. But if the fire is violent, crackling, and if the house seems about to be consumed, the opposite of these is portended.

XIV. When a man dreams that his bed is burning, this threatens damage, sickness, or unpleasantness for his wife. The significance is the same for a woman.

XV. The burning of household goods, involving their destruction in this manner, means damage or contrariety for the master of the house.

XVI. The burning of the lady's boudoir, or the larder, means sickness or bad news for the mistress of the house.

XVII. The burning of the kitchen means the loss of the cook, or one or more of the servants.

XVIII. COMPLETE DESTRUCTION OF THE SHOP BY FIRE MEANS LOSS OF POSSESSIONS.

XIX. THE DESTRUCTION OF THE FRONT WINDOWS BY FIRE PORTENDS THE LOSS OF A MALE RELATIVE; THE BACK WINDOWS THREATEN THE SAME EVENT IN RESPECT OF A FEMALE RELATIVE.

XX. THE BURNING OF DOORS MEANS GREAT MISFORTUNE FOR ONE OF THE FAMILY — POSSIBLY THE DREAMER HIMSELF.

XXI. TO DREAM THAT THE BEDPOSTS ARE ON FIRE BUT ARE NOT CONSUMED MEANS THAT THE MALE CHILDREN WILL BE FORTUNATE.

XXII. THE DESTRUCTION OF THE UPPER PART OF THE HOUSE BY FIRE DENOTES LOSS OF GOODS, LOSS OF A LAW CASE, OR LOSS OF FRIENDS.

XXIII. TO DREAM THAT ONE IS LIGHTING A FIRE AND THAT IT TAKES LIGHT AT ONCE, SIGNIFIES THE BIRTH OF FORTUNATE CHILDREN, WHO WILL DO HONOR TO THEIR MOTHER. THE LIGHTING OF A LAMP OR CANDLE CARRIES THE SAME MEANING.

XXIV. IF IT IS A MARRIED WOMAN WHO LIGHTS EITHER, THIS SHOWS THAT SHE IS WITH CHILD AND WILL BE HAPPILY DELIVERED OF A CHILD, WHOSE LIFE WILL BE FORTUNATE.

XXV. To dream of lighting a fire with great difficulty and that it goes out at once announces loss and vexation to the housewife and to the dreamer also.

XXVI. To see a house entirely burned down foretells loss, illness, or great vexation to the owner; to see a town so destroyed denotes famine, war, or pestilence therein.

XXVII. Weariness, injury, slander and loss of friends or at law are prognosticated when the sleeper sees his clothes consumed by fire.

XXVIII. The destruction of harvested wheat by fire means an epidemic disease; but if it should be on fire without being consumed, fertility and plenty may be expected by the dreamer.

XXIX. To see one's self on fire and suffering thereby signifies envy, displeasure, wrath, or quarreling.

XXX. To dream that one is carrying a torch of lighted straw in a public place signifies honor and success in business.

XXI. To dream of burning one's finger betokens envy and evil.

The Presages of Air

I. Those who dream that the air is serene and clear will be loved and esteemed by everyone; their enemies and those who envy them will seek reconciliation.

II. People who are accustomed to dream about air are considered to be of sanguine temperament.

III. To see the air pure and cloudless shows that what has been lost or stolen will be recovered, victory will be obtained over enemies, any pending lawsuit gained, the dreamer will be loved by all, and if he is about to travel, he will have a good journey or voyage.

IV. To see the air disturbed, cloudy, and darkened, forebodes sadness, sickness, melancholy, and difficulties in business, or, in a word, the opposite of all that is announced by clear air.

V. To dream of breathing soft and warm air indicates that the life and habits of the

SLEEPER ARE PURE, PEACEABLE, AND PLEASANT, THAT THE BUSINESS AND JOURNEYS UNDERTAKEN BY HIM WILL SUCCEED TO THE HEIGHT OF HIS WISHES.

VI. TO SEE RAIN FALLING GENTLY, WITHOUT STORM OR HIGH WIND, PROMISES GAIN IN HUSBANDRY.

VII. THE OPPOSITE OF THIS SPELLS THE OPPOSITE IN HUSBANDRY, WITH LOSS AND DAMAGE OF GOODS TO MERCHANTS.

VIII. TO DREAM OF LONG, HEAVY RAINS, HAIL, TEMPEST, AND LIGHTNING SIGNIFIES AMBITIONS, FATIGUES, DANGERS, AND LOSSES. FOR POOR PEOPLE, HOWEVER, IT INDICATES REPOSE.

IX. TO SEE SNOW AND ICE IN WINTER MEANS NOTHING; IT MAY WELL BE THE REMEMBRANCE OF YESTERDAY. BUT WHEN IT IS NOT IN THE WINTER, GOOD HARVEST AND ALL PLENTY ARE FORESHADOWED IN HUSBANDRY. ON THE OTHER HAND, FOR MERCHANTS AND BUSINESS MEN IT INTIMATES HINDRANCE IN COMMERCE AND IN JOURNEYS OR VOYAGES. FOR SOLDIERS IT MAY MEAN GOOD LUCK, OR ALTERNATIVELY UNCERTAINTY IN THEIR ENTERPRISES.

X. TO SEE HAIL IN DREAM PORTENDS TROUBLE AND SADNESS. IT MAY ALSO MEAN THAT THE

MOST SECRET AND HIDDEN THINGS WILL BE MADE MANIFEST.

XI. TO SEE A THUNDERBOLT FALL CLOSE BY ONE IN STILL WEATHER SIGNIFIES THAT THE DREAMER WILL HAVE TO TAKE FLIGHT, PERHAPS EVEN TO LEAVE HIS COUNTRY. THIS IS THE CASE ESPECIALLY WITH PEOPLE IN HIGH POSITIONS. IF THE BOLT FALLS ON ONE'S HEAD, OR ON HOUSES, IT SPELLS DANGER.

THE PRESAGES OF FIRE IN HEAVEN

I. TO SEE A GREAT BLAZE IN THE SKY DENOTES AGGRESSION ON THE PART OF ENEMIES, AS ALSO POVERTY, DESOLATION, AND FAMINE. ENEMIES WILL COME FROM THE QUARTER WHENCE THE FIRE DESCENDS. IF IT IS DARTING FIRE, FALLING IN SEVERAL PLACES, THE SIGN IS STILL MORE UNFAVORABLE.

II. TO SEE FLAMING TORCHES OR BRANCHES AND TREES OF FIRE COMING DOWN FROM HEAVEN MEANS WAR, QUARRELS, STERILITY, AND THE DREAMER IS MENACED WITH A WOUND ON THE HEAD, OR OTHER GREAT DANGER.

III. To see a still, pure, and bright fire in heaven is a menace to some prince or distinguished noble.

The Presages of Water

I. Those who are accustomed to dream of water and that they are immersed therein are of phlegmatic disposition; they may be subject to inflammations and colds.

II. To see very clear and quiet river water is a good augury, especially for travelers, litigants and judges.

III. To see it disturbed means that one is threatened by someone in a high place, or may fall into disgrace with one's master. Litigants will be in difficulties and likely to be judged wrongly.

IV. To dream that one is in a rapid river and cannot get out threatens danger for the dreamer, or sickness, or a protracted lawsuit.

V. To dream that one is swimming in a great river signifies imminent peril.

VI. TO SEE A CLEAR RIVER GLIDING PAST ONE'S CHAMBER PROGNOSTICATES THE COMING OF SOME WEALTHY AND GENEROUS PERSON, WHO WILL BRING PROFIT TO THE DREAMER; BUT IF THE WATER IS TROUBLED AND SEEMS TO BE DAMAGING THE FURNITURE OF THE ROOM, THIS MEANS TURMOIL AND DISORDER, OCCASIONED BY ENEMIES OF THOSE WHO DWELL IN THE HOUSE.

VII. A RICH MAN WHO DREAMS THAT A CLEAR STREAM IS RUNNING NEAR HIS HOUSE WILL SOON BE IN POSSESSION OF SOME LUCRATIVE AND HONORABLE EMPLOYMENT, AND WILL BE THE MAINSTAY OF THE UNFORTUNATE.

VIII. TO SEE A STREAM OF TROUBLED WATER SIGNIFIES LOSS AND DAMAGE BY FIRE, LAWSUITS, OR ENEMIES.

IX. TO SEE A WELL FULL OF EXCELLENT WATER, IN A MEADOW IS A FAVORABLE SIGN. HE WHO DREAMS IT WILL MAKE GOOD PURCHASES; HE WILL MARRY VERY SOON, IF HE HAS NOT DONE SO ALREADY, AND WILL HAVE GOOD AND OBEDIENT CHILDREN.

X. TO SEE A WELL OVERFLOWING WITH WATER PREDICTS LOSS OF GOODS, OR SOME GREAT MISFORTUNE WHICH WILL BEFALL A RELATION OF

THE DREAMER. IN THE CASE OF A WOMAN, SHE IS MENACED WITH THE LOSS OF PART OF HER PROPERTY.

XI. TO DREAM OF A SMALL POND MEANS THAT A MAN WILL BE LOVED BY A BEAUTIFUL WOMAN; BUT IF IT IS A WOMAN WHO DREAMS, SHE WILL OBTAIN THAT WHICH SHE DESIRES.

XII. TO BE IN A BOAT ON A RIVER, LAKE, OR POND, WHERE THE WATER IS CLEAR, IS A SIGN OF JOY, PROSPERITY, AND SUCCESS IN BUSINESS OR OCCUPATION.

XIII. TO SEE STREAMS OR FOUNTAINS OF CLEAR, RUNNING WATER PRESAGES THE RAPID CURE OF A SICK DREAMER; BUT IF THE WATER IS FOUL OR DISTURBED, THIS SIGNIFIES SLOW RECOVERY.

XIV. IF A YOUNG MAN DREAMS THAT HE IS DRAWING CLEAR WATER FROM A WELL, IT SIGNIFIES THAT HE WILL BE MARRIED PRESENTLY TO A BEAUTIFUL GIRL, WHO WILL BRING HIM A DOWRY. BUT IF THE WATER IS TROUBLED, HE WILL EXPERIENCE DIFFICULTY IN HIS COURTSHIP.

XV. IF HE DREAMS THAT HE IS GIVING OTHERS TO DRINK FROM CLEAR WELL WATER, THIS BEARS WITNESS THAT HE WILL ENRICH THEM; BUT IF THE

WATER IS TROUBLED, HE WILL PROVE A CAUSE OF LOSS TO THEM.

XVI. TO DREAM THAT ONE'S BROOK, POOL, OR SPRING IS DRIED UP PRESAGES IMPAIRED FORTUNE.

XVII. TO DREAM OF WATER SPRINGING UP IN A PLACE WHICH IS UNLIKELY TO ALL APPEARANCE PROMISES ANXIETIES, CARE, AND AFFLICTION.

XVIII. TO DREAM THAT ONE DRAWS SUCH WATER MEANS THAT THE EVIL FORTUNE WILL CONTINUE FOR A LONGER PERIOD.

XIX. TO DREAM THAT SUCH WATER CEASES TO FLOW MEANS AN END OF THE TROUBLE.

XX. TO DRINK WARM WATER ANNOUNCES MISCHANCE OCCASIONED BY ENEMIES; THE CONSEQUENT INCONVENIENCE WILL BE MORE OR LESS IN PROPORTION TO THE WARMTH OF THE WATER. COLD WATER PRESAGES GOOD THINGS; WARM OR BOILING WATER, THINGS THAT ARE EVIL.

XXI. TO SEE A BATH MEANS PAIN OR AFFLICTION.

XXII. TO DREAM OF TAKING A BATH AND FINDING IT TOO HOT MEANS DISPLEASURE AND AFFLICTION OCCASIONED BY RELATIVES. HERE ALSO THE AMOUNT OF TROUBLE IS REGULATED BY THE TEMPERATURE OF THE WATER.

XXIII. To dream of undressing without entering the bath means that the distress to come will be transient.

XXIV. To dream of taking a bath and finding it too cold has the same significance as the opposite extreme; but if it is temperate, the omen is good.

XXV. To dream of carrying water in a broken vessel, which cannot contain it, denotes loss and other damage, deception on the part of those who have been entrusted with our goods and money, or robbery by an unknown person.

XXVI. If the water so drawn is not lost, the possessions will be saved with difficulty; if part is spilt, a partial loss may be expected.

XXVII. If the dreamer buries vessel and water in the ground, a substantial loss is likely.

XXVIII. To be given in sleep a glass full of water portends that the dreamer will soon be married and that his wife will bear him children. Glass always signifies wife or woman; water means abundance, increase, and multiplication.

XXIX. If the glass is broken it denotes the loss of several friends.

XXX. If a preacher dreams that he gives his congregation clear water to drink, this means that the word of God will come forth from his lips and will be the instrument of their salvation.

XXXI. If the water is clouded, he will fail to turn their hearts.

XXXI. To dream of spilling water in one's own house foreshows loss and affliction, the extent of these being in proportion to the quantity of water.

Presages of Life at Sea

I. He who dreams that he is on board ship, and is neither nervous nor otherwise disturbed, will have joy in the success of his affairs; but if the water is stirred by tempest he may look for the opposite.

II. To be on a boat or ship which seems about to founder is a sign of peril, unless the

DREAMER IS IN CAPTIVITY, WHEN IT WILL BE A TOKEN OF COMING LIBERTY.

III. TO SEE AN ANCHOR SIGNIFIES SAFETY AND CERTAIN HOPE.

IV. TO DREAM OF SHIP'S RIGGING BETOKENS NEWS OF DEBTORS OR OF PERSONS IN ONE'S EMPLOYMENT.

V. TO SEE THE OCEAN BLUE AND RIPPLING SLIGHTLY SIGNIFIES JOY AND MEANS OF SUCCESS IN BUSINESS.

VI. IF THE SEA IS UTTERLY BECALMED, IT MEANS DELAY AND PROTRACTION.

VII. IF IT IS TOSSED BY TEMPEST, THERE IS PROMISE OF AFFLICTION, LOSS, AND ADVERSITY.

THE PRESAGES OF EARTH

I. HE WHO DREAMS THAT HE HAS BEEN GIVEN A PLEASANT PIECE OF GROUND WILL HAVE A HANDSOME WIFE, WHOSE GOOD LOOKS WILL CORRESPOND TO THE BEAUTY OF THE LAND WHICH HAS BECOME HIS OWN IN SLEEP.

II. IF IT IS A SPACIOUS AREA, HAVING GARDENS, SPRINGS, MEADOWS, COPPICES, AND ABUNDANT ORCHARD, THIS MEANS THAT HIS WIFE WILL BE PURE

AND PRUDENT, AS WELL AS BEAUTIFUL, AND THAT THEY WILL HAVE HANDSOME CHILDREN.

III. To see the land covered with wheat bespeaks money and profit, with needful care and toil.

IV. To see it covered with vegetables means trouble and affliction.

V. To see it covered with millet foretells great wealth, wealth acquired without difficulty and with joy in the winning.

VI. When these dreams are experienced by a wise man, they promise riches and contentment of the mind.

VII. To see black earth forecasts sadness, melancholy, and credulous weakness.

VIII. To dream that the earth trembles signifies danger in business matters.

IX. To dream of a great earthquake means that the king or government of the country will perform some public act which will gratify all the people.

X. A slight earthquake presages loss by a lawsuit affecting the house in which the dreamer is sleeping.

XI. To dream that walls, doors, and roofs collapse in consequence of an earthquake denotes ruination for the owners of the building.

XII. If a king or prince dreams that his palace or throne is cast down by an earthquake, he may expect great adversity.

XIII. To dream that a mountain has fallen into a plain means the downfall of some great peer or noble.

XIV. To dream that a town of our acquaintance is engulfed by an earthquake is a sign of war and famine; but if the town is unknown to the dreamer, the nation to which it belongs will perish through the same causes.

XV. To kiss the earth means sorrow and humiliation.

XVI. To dream of falling into a great ditch, or down a precipice, portends great injuries, or serious danger, or that our possessions are menaced by fire through the action of an incendiary.

XVII. To dream that one is in the meadows is a good sign for agriculturists and shepherds, but it prognosticates an impediment in business for other persons.

XVIII. To dream that one is traveling along a good road, and one that is straight and pleasant, signifies joy, prosperity, success; but a bad road is to be interpreted in the opposite sense.

Presages of Plants
Flowers

I. To hold and inhale the scent of flowers in their proper season means joy, pleasure, and consolation.

II. But if they are out of season, white flowers mean impediment in respect of designs and failure in enterprises; yellow flowers mean less serious impediments; red flowers mean that either impediments are slight or that success may be expected.

III. To hold and inhale the scent of roses in season is a good sign for everyone, except those who are ill or are in hiding through

FEAR. THESE ARE EITHER IN DANGER OF RECOVERING SLOWLY OR OF BEING FOUND OUT.

IV. THE OPPOSITE OF ALL THIS IS TO BE UNDERSTOOD IF THE ROSES ARE OUT OF SEASON, SO THEREFORE WHILE IT IS A BAD OMEN IN GENERAL, IT PROMISES QUICK RECOVERY TO THE SICK AND A SAFE ASYLUM FOR THOSE DESIRING CONCEALMENT.

V. TO DREAM OF LILIES OUT OF SEASON IS A PLEDGE OF HOPES REALIZED.

VI. IF A WOMEN SHOULD DREAM OF LAUREL, OLIVE, AND PALM TREES, IT MEANS THAT SHE WILL BEAR CHILDREN, SUPPOSING THAT SHE IS ALREADY MARRIED.

VII. IF THEY ARE SEEN IN DREAM BY A MAIDEN, IT IS A SIGN OF HER SPEEDY MARRIAGE.

VIII. IF THEY ARE SEEN IN DREAM BY A MAN, THEY DENOTE FRIENDSHIP, JOY, PROSPERITY, ABUNDANCE, AND GREAT SUCCESS IN UNDERTAKINGS.

THE HERB-GARDEN

I. TO DREAM OF SMELLING SWEET MARJORAM, HYSSOP, ROSEMARY, SAGE AND HERBS OF THIS KIND PRESAGES TOIL, SADNESS, AND WEAKNESS, EXCEPT FOR MEDICAL MEN, AND IT IS FAVORABLE IN THEIR CASE.

II. To dream of eating or smelling herbs of strong scent—radishes, garlic, onions, leeks, and so forth—augurs the disclosure of hidden things and quarrels with servants.

III. To dream of herbs which are used in salads and other vegetables which can be eaten uncooked, as lettuce, sorrel, and purslain, signifies afflictions and difficulties in business.

IV. To eat medicinal herbs, like bugloss, fumitory, and borage, promises liberation from weariness and expedition in business affairs.

V. To dream of eating cabbages, colewort, or kale foretells vexation.

VI. Turnips and cucumbers symbolize vain hopes.

VII. Some of the herbalists have ruled that if sick people dream of eating melons and cucumbers, this is a prediction of their recovery.

WHEAT AND OTHER CEREALS

I. To see ears of harvested corn in sleep, and to pluck some of them, typifies profit and riches.

II. To see much corn in sheaves predicts an abundance of good things and benefit for the dreamer.

III. To see a few sheaves only means dearth and necessity.

IV. To dream of eating white wheaten bread portends profit to those who are rich, but detriment to the poor.

V. To dream of eating black bread means profit to the poor and loss to those who are rich.

VI. To dream of eating a barley-stew is a sign of gain and profit.

VII. To see a barn full of corn is a pledge of marriage with a rich woman, success in a suit at law, inheritance of landed estate, wealth gained by trading, gift, or otherwise, as well as feasts and rejoicings.

VIII. To dream of eating well-cooked peas denotes felicity and great acceleration in business things.

IX. To eat beans in sleep denotes noise and dissension.

X. To dream of lentils signifies corruption.

XI. To dream of rice signifies abundance, or obstruction.

XII. To dream of dry millet means want and poverty.

XIII. To see or eat mustard-seed is a bad sign, except for doctors, to whom the dream is favorable.

TREES AND FRUITS

I. To see a fine oak in dream promises wealth, profit, and long life.

II. To see an olive-tree bearing olives denotes peace, mildness, concord, freedom, dignity, and the enjoyment of lawful things desired by the heart.

III. To dream of picking up fallen olives signifies pain and labor.

IV. To see a laurel is the sign of victory and pleasure, and in the case of a married man it promises some inheritance through his wife.

V. To see a cypress denotes vexations, afflictions, and delay in business matters.

VI. To see a pine, medlar, or service-tree spells idleness.

VII. To see apple-trees and eat sweet apples means joy, pleasure, and recreation, above all for women and maids.

VIII. To eat almonds, walnuts, and hazelnuts is an omen of troubles and difficulties.

IX. To see figs in their season is a sign of joy and pleasure, but it is the opposite if they are out of season.

X. To see a vine typifies abundance, riches, and fruitfulness.

XI. To eat ripe grapes speaks of joy and profit.

XII. To see and partake of oranges threatens wounding, pains, and vexations.

XIII. Mulberries have the same significance.

XIV. To see and to eat peaches or apricots in season is a pledge of contentment, health, and enjoyment.

XV. If they are out of season, they speak of vain hopes and failure in business.

XVI. To see and to eat ripe pears foretells joy and pleasure, but it is the reverse if they are sour and wild.

XVII. To see a mulberry-tree in dream means a wealth of good things, including a promise of children.

XVIII. To find hidden nuts means the discovery of a treasure.

XIX. To see mulberry-trees, almond-trees and to partake of their fruit, is a sign of joy, consolation and diversion; but if they are withered, barren, leafless, fallen, burnt or blasted by lightning, they foretell weariness, fear, displeasure and suffering.

XX. To gather the fruit of a pomegranate-tree means that the dreamer will be enriched by a man of wealth; but if the fruit is not ripe it denotes illness or trouble occasioned by the wicked.

XXI. To dream of gathering fruits and finding them rotten is a sign of adversity or the loss of children.

XXII. To dream that one has climbed a great tree speaks of approaching elevation to some degree of dignity and that others will be under our rule.

XXIII. TO DREAM OF FALLING FROM A TREE AND BEING SCRATCHED BY BRAMBLES, OR HURT IN SOME OTHER MANNER, PORTENDS THE LOSS OF FAVOR WITH INFLUENTIAL PERSONS.

PRESAGES OF BIRDS AND INSECTS

I. TO DREAM OF AN EAGLE IN A HIGH PLACE, OR FLYING THROUGH THE MIDHEAVEN IS GOOD FOR THOSE WHO ARE STARTING ON SOME GREAT UNDERTAKING, ESPECIALLY IN MILITARY AFFAIRS.

II. TO DREAM OF AN EAGLE SWOOPING DOWN ON ONE'S HEAD IS A SIGN OF ILLNESS.

III. TO DREAM OF BEING CARRIED OFF BY AN EAGLE HAS THE SAME IMPORT.

IV. IF A WOMAN GIVES BIRTH TO AN EAGLE IN DREAM, THIS PREDICTS THAT SHE WILL BEAR A CHILD WHO WILL ATTAIN GREATNESS AND WILL RULE OTHERS.

V. TO SEE A DEAD EAGLE MEANS LOSS TO THOSE IN HIGH PLACES AND GAIN FOR THOSE IN POVERTY.

VI. TO SEE BIRDS OF PREY OR THOSE USED IN HAWKING SIGNIFIES INCREASE OF FORTUNE AND

HONOR FOR THE RICH AND SOME CHANGE OF POSITION FOR THE POOR.

VII. TO SEE A RAVEN IN SLEEP IS A BAD SIGN AND ABOVE ALL FOR A HUSBAND, WHO MAY HAVE CAUSE FOR GRAVE SELF-REPROACH. IN THE CASE OF A WIFE OR WOMAN IT PROGNOSTICATES DEEP AFFLICTION.

VIII. TO SEE A ROOK OR CARRION-CROW SIGNIFIES DISPATCH IN BUSINESS MATTERS.

IX. TO SEE A STARLING PORTENDS A SLIGHT DISPLEASURE.

X. TO SEE DOVES IS A GOOD SIGN. THERE WILL BE JOY AND PLEASURE IN THE HOUSE AND SUCCESS IN BUSINESS.

XI. TO SEE CRANES OR STORKS FLOCKING THROUGH THE AIR MEANS THE APPROACH OF ENEMIES OR ENVIOUS RELATIONS. IN WINTER THEY DENOTE BAD WEATHER.

XII. TO SEE TWO STORKS TOGETHER PROMISES MARRIAGE AND BIRTH OF CHILDREN, WHO WILL BE GOOD AND PROFITABLE TO THEIR PARENTS.

XIII. TO SEE A SWAN IS THE PLEDGE OF COMING GAYETY AND THE REVELATION OF SECRET THINGS; IT ALSO MEANS HEALTH TO THE DREAMER.

XIV. TO SEE A SINGING SWAN IS OF EVIL AUGURY.

XV. To see a swallow is the gage of a good wife, good news and of blessing on one's own home.

XVI. To see a nightingale has the same meanings.

XVII. To see bees signifies gain for the country people and loss for the rich.

XVIII. To dream that bees have made their honey in some part of the house speaks of dignity, eloquence and success in business.

XIX. To dream of being stung by flies, especially wasps, portends weariness and troubles caused by the envious.

XX. To see many birds foretells assemblies and lawsuits.

XXI. To hear a cock crow announces joy and prosperity.

XXII. To see two cocks fighting means feud and warfare.

XXIII. To see a peacock means a beautiful and wealthy wife, who is a favorite with the great of this world.

XXIV. To see a hen with its chickens presages loss and damage.

XXV. To see a capon or hear a hen crow is significant of sadness and weariness.

XXVI. To see partridges is an omen of dealing with unscrupulous, ungrateful and evil women.

XXVII. Quails are prophetic of bad news by sea. disputes, bickerings, thieveries, ambushes and treason.

XXVIII. All night-birds, as screech-owl, common owl, or bat, are of evil augury. Those who see them in dreams should enter into no new undertaking on the following day.

XXIX. To dream of eggs promises gain; but if they are in very great numbers, anxiety and litigation may be expected.

XXX. Grasshoppers, may-bugs, crickets and cicadas signify great talkers, bad musicians, and needy people who plunder the country-side. This dream offers no good prospect to the sleeper, at least during the first day following.

XXXI. To see scorpions or caterpillars presages trouble occasioned by the envious.

XXXII. TO DREAM OF EARTH-WORMS DENOTES THAT ENEMIES ARE SEEKING TO TAKE US BY SURPRISE AND INJURE US.

PRESAGES FROM REPTILES AND FISHES

I. TO DREAM OF A DRAGON MEANS A MEETING WITH SOME INFLUENTIAL PERSON, WITH ONE'S MASTER, OR WITH A MAGISTRATE.

II. TO SEE A SERPENT TWISTING AND COILING DENOTES THAT ONE HAS ENEMIES. IT STANDS FOR HATE AND SICKNESS.

III. TO SEE A SERPENT OTHERWISE SIGNIFIES TREASON ON THE PART OF A WOMAN.

IV. TO DREAM THAT ONE DESTROYS A SERPENT SIGNIFIES VICTORY OVER ENEMIES AND JEALOUS PEOPLE.

V. TO SEE BASILISKS AND LIZARDS PROMISES LOSS OR OPPOSITION ARISING FROM SECRET ENEMIES.

VI. FROGS SIGNIFY FLATTERERS, BABBLERS AND IGNORANT PERSONS.

VII. TO DREAM OF CATCHING LARGE FISH IS A TOKEN OF PROFIT IN PROPORTION TO THE QUANTITY TAKEN.

VIII. TO CATCH SMALL FISH IS A MARK OF COMING SADNESS.

IX. TO SEE FISH OF MANY COLORS PROMISES RECOVERY TO THE SICK, BUT TO THOSE WHO ARE WELL IT MEANS INJURIES, QUARRELS, OR PAINS.

X. TO EAT BIG FISH IN A DREAM IS AN OMEN OF INFLAMMATION, COLDS AND DEPRESSION.

XI. TO DREAM OF FISHING-NETS IS A SIGN OF RAIN OR SOME OTHER CHANGE IN THE WEATHER.

XII. TO SEE DEAD FISH IN THE SEA IS A PORTENT OF VAIN HOPES.

VIII. IF A WOMAN WHO IS WITH CHILD DREAMS OF GIVING BIRTH TO A FISH, HER ACTUAL OFFSPRING WILL BE A FINE CHILD WHO WILL ATTAIN LENGTH OF DAYS.

THE PRESAGES OF BEASTS

I. HE WHO SEES A LION IN HIS SLEEP WILL SPEAK EITHER TO HIS SOVEREIGN OR TO SOME ILLUSTRIOUS SOLDIER.

II. TO DREAM OF FIGHTING WITH A LION IS THE PLEDGE OF A STRUGGLE WITH SOME COURAGEOUS

OPPONENT; AND IF A VICTORY IS GAINED IN THE SLEEP-LIFE, IT WILL BE GAINED IN THE LIFE OF DAY.

III. TO RIDE ON THE BACK OF A LION SIGNIFIES PRINCELY PROTECTION, OR AT LEAST THAT OF AN INFLUENTIAL PERSON.

IV. TO BE AFRAID OF A LION IN SLEEP IS TO HAVE MERITED THE ROYAL DISPLEASURE, OR THAT OF SOME GREAT PERSON.

V. HE WHO DREAMS OF EATING LION'S FLESH WILL BE ENRICHED AND COVERED WITH HONORS.

VI. TO DREAM OF FINDING THE HIDE, LIVER OR MARROW OF A LION MEANS THAT ONE IN HIGH PLACE WILL OBTAIN THE TREASURES OF HIS ENEMIES AND THAT AN ORDINARY PERSON WILL GROW RICH IN A SHORT TIME.

VII. IF A KING DREAMS THAT HE IS CARRIED OFF BOUND BY A LION, HE WILL BE MADE A PRISONER.

VIII. IF HE DREAMS THAT A LIONESS AND HER CUBS ARE IN HIS PALACE, THIS SIGNIFIES THAT THE QUEEN AND THE ROYAL CHILDREN WILL CAUSE HIM MUCH SATISFACTION.

IX. DREAMS ABOUT LEOPARDS ARE OF THE SAME SIGNIFICANCE AS THOSE CONCERNING LIONS, ALLOWANCE BEING MADE FOR THE CRAFT OF THE

FORMER BEASTS AND FOR THE GENEROUS QUALITIES ASCRIBED TO THE LATTER.

X. TO DREAM OF AN ELEPHANT STANDS FOR FEAR AND DANGER, BUT THE TESTIMONY OF INTERPRETERS DIFFERS ON THIS POINT. IT IS SAID ALSO TO DENOTE A RICH MAN WHO MAY BRING FORTUNE TO THE DREAMER.

XI. TO DREAM OF RIDING ON AN ELEPHANT MAY BE A PRESAGE OF APPROACHING ILLNESS.

XII. TO DREAM OF GIVING FOOD AND DRINK TO AN ELEPHANT MEANS ENTRANCE INTO THE SERVICE OF SOME GREAT PERSONAGE, TO THE PROFIT OF THE DREAMER.

XIII. TO SEE A BEAR SIGNIFIES AN ENEMY WHO IS WEALTHY AND POWERFUL, BUT AWKWARD, RIDICULOUS AND INSOLENT.

XIV. TO DREAM OF OVERCOMING A WOLF MEANS TRIUMPH OVER AN AVARICIOUS, CRUEL AND DISLOYAL FOE.

XV. TO BE BITTEN BY A WOLF HAS THE CONTRARY MEANING.

XVI. TO DREAM OF COMBATING A FOX INDICATES A DISPUTE WITH A CRAFTY AND ACUTE ENEMY.

XVII. HE WHO DREAMS THAT HE HAS A TAME FOX AT HOME WILL FALL IN LOVE WITH AN EVIL WOMAN AND BE A SLAVE TO HER; OR ALTERNATIVELY, HE WILL TRUST A DOMESTIC WHO WILL ABUSE HIS GOODNESS.

XVIII. TO SEE LYNXES, MARTENS OR WEASELS WILL BEAR A SIMILAR INTERPRETATION.

XIX. TO DREAM OF CHASING OR CAPTURING A WILD BOAR MEANS HUNTING OR CORNERING AN ENEMY POSSESSED OF THAT ANIMAL'S QUALITIES, WHICH ARE RAGE AND CRUELTY.

XX. TO DREAM OF CARRYING THE HEAD OF A WILD BOAR RECENTLY TAKEN IN THE CHASE MEANS SPEEDY TRIUMPH OVER OUR MOST POWERFUL ENEMY.

XXI. WHEN SWINE ARE BEHELD IN DREAM THEY STAND FOR IDLE AND GOOD FOR NOTHING PEOPLE, WHO SEEK TO LIVE AT THEIR EASE BY PREYING ON OTHERS. THEY ALSO REPRESENT MISERS.

XXII. TO DREAM ABOUT DOGS THAT BELONG TO US DENOTES FAITH, COURAGE AND AFFECTION IN FRIENDS.

XXIII. TO DREAM OF STRANGE DOGS SIGNIFIES DANGEROUS ENÉMIES.

XXIV. To dream that a barking dog is rending our clothes gives warning of an enemy in some lower walk of life who is slandering and trying to disgrace us.

XXV. The cat is supposed to stand for a clever thief, and to dream of fighting with a cat or destroying one means casting a thief into prison or in some way putting an end to his activities.

XXVI. To dream of having a cat's skin means that the thief's spoil will come into our hands.

XXVII. To dream of being scratched by a cat signifies illness or afflictions.

XXVIII. To dream of monkeys is significant of malicious, weak, strange and unknown enemies.

XXIX. To dream of killing a stag and taking its horns and hide means inheritance from an aged person, or the defeat of deceptive, cowardly and retreating enemies.

XXX. To see ourselves owners of much cattle, horses and so forth, signifies wealth and plenty.

XXXI. To dream of being butted by a ram threatens punishment by law.

XXXII. An ass seen in sleep means a good servant who is profitable to his master, or else an inept and ignorant fellow.

XXXIII. To see a mule in dream is a promise of contrariety.

XXXIV. To dream of an ox is to dream of a faithful servant.

XXXV. To dream of a bull signifies some person of importance, and as the bull does good or otherwise to us in our sleep so will his representative in waking life.

XXXVI. It is always of good augury to see or get possession of a horse and also to be riding on one.

XXXVII. To dream of riding a fine horse, full of courage and activity, and well harnessed, means marriage with a handsome woman, wealthy and of high birth; but this is on condition that the horse is understood to be ours. If it belongs to another, joy, honor and possessions will come to us through an unknown woman.

XXXVIII. HE WHO DREAMS OF RIDING HORSE OR MARE OVER A HARD AND RUGGED ROAD, WITHOUT THE ANIMAL STUMBLING, WILL OBTAIN HONOR, DIGNITY AND RENOWN.

XXXIX. TO BE CARRIED BY A LONG-TAILED HORSE MEANS REINFORCEMENT OF FRIENDS WHO WILL HELP OUR ENTERPRISES.

XL. IF THE HORSE LIMPS IN OUR DREAM, OBSTACLES WILL INTERFERE WITH OUR DESIGN.

XLI. TO DREAM THAT SOMEONE IS RIDING ONE OF OUR HORSES AGAINST OUR WILL DENOTES AN ATTEMPT TO SEDUCE ONE OF OUR SERVANTS.

XLII. OTHER INTERPRETERS SAY THAT TO RIDE A BOLD AND FIERY HORSE IS A PLEDGE THAT THE DREAMER WILL BE HONORED BY THE PUBLIC AND ESTEEMED BY THE GREAT.

XLIII. IF THE RIDER SPURS SUCH A HORSE AND HAS HIM FULLY UNDER CONTROL HE WILL BE ADVANCED IN OFFICES AND DIGNITIES. HIS HONORS WILL BE IN PROPORTION TO HIS PERFORMANCE.

XLIV. IN THE DREAMS OF KINGS, A WHITE HORSE HAS REFERENCE TO THE PERSON OF THE COMING QUEEN AND PROMISES THAT SHE WILL BE BEAUTIFUL AND GOOD.

XLV. A BLACK HORSE IN THE SAME CASE REFERS TO A RICH BUT WICKED WOMAN.

XLVI. TO DREAM THAT A YOUNG, FRISKY AND WELL-HARNESSED MARE COMES INTO ONE'S HOUSE SIGNIFIES SPEEDY MARRIAGE WITH A FAIR, YOUNG AND WEALTHY LADY, BY WHOM OUR HAPPINESS WILL BE INSURED. BUT IF THE MARE HAVE NO SADDLE AND IS NOT GOOD TO LOOK AT, A FEMALE SERVANT IS SIGNIFIED, OR A MISTRESS WHO WILL BRING NOTHING.

XLVII. TO BE RIDING THROUGH THE STREETS OF A LARGE TOWN, FOLLOWED BY A CHEERING CROWD, PRESAGES THAT THE DREAMER WILL BE AT THE HEAD OF SOME POPULAR FACTION.

PRESAGES OF PERFUMES

I. TO DREAM THAT ONE'S HEAD IS PERFUMED WITH OILS, ESSENCES OR POWDERS SIGNIFIES GREAT SELF-ESTEEM AND PRIDE EXHIBITED TO OTHERS. IN THE CASE OF A WOMAN SHE WILL GLORY IN THE EXERCISE OF POWER.

II. To dream of being adorned and to think that one is looking at one's best speaks of coming danger, through illness or otherwise.

III. The Easterns say that to dream of being perfumed means that we shall be esteemed by our neighbors and agreeable to all about us.

IV. He who dreams of exuding bad odors will soon prove hateful to others.

V. He who dreams that he has been presented with aromatic or scented waters will have good news in proportion to the quality and extent of the gifts received in sleep; he will make a substantial gain and acquire honors.

VI. He who dreams of distributing scents to his friends will have news advantageous to himself and those about him.

Presages of Wounds

I. To dream of being wounded by a sword and like to die thereof signifies that the sleep-victim will have pleasures and benefactions from the hand of the person who has appeared to maim him, and that they will be

IN PROPORTION TO THE NUMBER AND SEVERITY OF THE BLOWS.

II. TO BE SO WOUNDED BY A PERSON IN HIGH PLACE, AND ESPECIALLY BY A RULER OF THE LAND, MEANS BENEFITS FROM THAT PERSON IN THE PROPORTION ABOVE MENTIONED.

III. IF A WOMAN IS WOUNDED IN DREAM OR STRIKES WITH THE SWORD IN SELF-DEFENSE, OR IN SOME OTHER GOOD CAUSE, SHE WILL RECEIVE HONORS AND, IF SHE BE MARRIED, WILL GIVE BIRTH TO A MALE CHILD.

IV. IF A ROYAL PERSON, OR SOMEONE IN HIGH COMMAND, IS STRUCK UPSTANDING BY SWORD OR KNIFE, AND IF THE ATTACKING PARTY BE ONE OF MEAN ESTATE, THE DREAMER IS IN DANGER OF BEING KILLED OR CAST DOWN FROM HIS HIGH POSITION.

PRESAGES OF HAIR

I. IF A MAN DREAMS THAT HIS HAIR IS LONG LIKE A WOMAN'S, THIS DENOTES POLTROONERY AND EFFEMINACY, OR OTHERWISE, DECEPTION BY A WOMAN.

II. To see a woman without hair signifies famine, poverty and sickness.

III. To see a hairless man has the opposite meaning.

IV. To see mixed hair is an omen of pain and weariness, sometimes of injuries and quarrels.

V. To see very black hair, which is also short and frizzled, promises suffering and sadness.

VI. To dream of combing one's hair and being unable to draw the comb through announces long toil and a suit at law.

VII. To see a head with the hair well-dressed means friendship and freedom from bad business.

VIII. He who dreams that his beard or head is being shaved will be in danger of losing a substantial part of his possessions, or of falling ill, or of losing one of whom he is fond.

IX. To see hair fall off signifies weariness and loss of goods.

X. The soldier who dreams that his hair is very good and abundant will become terrible to his enemies, supposing that he is a person

IN COMMAND, WILL ACQUIRE A GREAT REPUTATION AND WILL SUBJECT MANY PROVINCES.

XI. TO DREAM THAT ONE'S HAIR HAS WHITENED MEANS THAT POSSESSIONS WILL DIMINISH, ALMOST TO A VANISHING POINT.

XII. TO DREAM THAT IT HAS GROWN LONGER AND DARKER MEANS INCREASE OF HONORS AND RICHES.

XIII. TO DREAM THAT THE HAIR OF ONE'S BEARD IS CUT OR TORN OFF IS GENERALLY OF EVIL OMEN AND ESPECIALLY AS REGARDS LOSS OF GOODS.

XIV. TO DREAM THAT ONE'S BEARD HAS GROWN UNUSUALLY MEANS INCREASE OF MONEY.

XV. TO DREAM THAT ONE'S HAIR HAS BECOME THINNER IS A SIGN OF POVERTY AND AFFLICTION.

PRESAGES OF THE VISAGE
THE FOREHEAD

I. TO DREAM THAT ONE HAS A BROAD FOREHEAD SYMBOLIZES A BROAD MIND, AND IF IT IS ALSO HIGH, THIS IS A MARK OF GOOD JUDGMENT, AS WELL AS OF POWER AND WEALTH.

II. TO DREAM THAT ONE HAS A FRONT OF BRASS TESTIFIES TO IRRECONCILABLE HATRED OF ENEMIES.

III. To dream that one's head is broken or wounded gives warning of riches discovered and in danger of being lost. It denotes also fear and apprehension.

IV. To dream that one has a bulky and fleshy forehead means facility of speech, force and constancy.

COMPLEXION

I. To dream that one has a wife with a graceful head and fair countenance promises joy, contentment and safety.

II. If a woman sees a handsome man in her sleep, the meaning is similar.

III. To see an unknown man of brown complexion signifies honor and glory.

IV. To see a very dark woman threatens a dangerous illness.

V. To see an unknown woman with long and beautiful hair is a promise of friendship, joy and prosperity.

VI. To see a fresh and radiant face is a sign of friendship.

VII. To see an emaciated and pallid face portends weariness and poverty.

EYEBROWS AND EYELASHES

I. To dream that one's eyebrows and lashes have grown thicker and more beautiful is a sign of being generally honored and esteemed, fortunate in love and destined to become rich.

II. To dream that they have come off carries the contrary meaning.

THE NOSE

I. To dream that one's nose has grown larger is a promise of wealth, power, increased sagacity and of welcome on the part of the great.

II. To dream that one has no nose signifies the opposite of this.

III. To dream that one has two noses means strife and discord.

IV. To dream of one's nose becoming so large that it is deformed and hideous to view promises prosperity and abundance, but not popularity.

V. To dream that one's nose is obstructed, so that nothing can be smelt, is to be in danger of deception by a friend or servant.

VI. In the case of a woman, she must be on her guard, or she may be betrayed.

THE EARS

I. To dream of being all ears means that we shall win the friendship of servants and those about us, that we shall be served and obeyed faithfully.

II. To dream of washing the ears bears the same interpretation as the above.

III. To dream that our ears are hung with wheat is a sign of inheritance from relations.

IV. To dream of having ass's ears signifies service.

V. To dream of having lion's ears, or those of some other savage beast, promises treason on the part of enemies and jealous people.

VI. If anyone dreams that his ears are larger and finer than usual, he will find that the person to whom he has communicated his secrets will attain honor and prosperity.

VII. To have an ear wounded or cloven in dream portends our betrayal by someone

BELONGING TO OUR FAMILY OR CIRCLE AND TO WHOM OUR SECRETS HAVE BEEN ENTRUSTED.

VIII. TO DREAM THAT AN EAR HAS BEEN CUT OFF COMPLETELY MEANS THAT WE SHALL BE DEPRIVED OF THE FRIENDSHIP OF THOSE WHO ARE NEAR TO US.

IX. TO DREAM THAT ONE'S EARS ARE STOPPED UP INTIMATES A CHANGE IN OUR PLANS AND THAT WE SHALL DECEIVE THOSE WHO DEPEND UPON US.

X. IN THE CASE OF A WOMAN, SHE IS IN DANGER OF SEDUCTION.

THE EYES

I. HE WHO DREAMS OF LOSING HIS SIGHT WILL NOT KEEP HIS PROMISE. OTHERWISE, HE IS IN DANGER OF ILLNESS, OF SEEING HIS FRIENDS NO MORE, OR OF HIS CHILD FALLING ILL.

II. TO DREAM THAT ONE'S EYES ARE BLEARY MEANS THE COMMISSION OF A GRAVE FAULT, FOLLOWED BY REPENTANCE. IT MAY MEAN ALSO THE LOSS OF PART OF ONE'S PROPERTY.

III. IT IS GOOD TO DREAM THAT OUR SIGHT IS KEEN AND CLEAR; IT IS A PROMISE OF PROSPERITY IN ENTERPRISE.

IV. TO DREAM THAT OUR SIGHT IS SHORT AND DIM SIGNIFIES WANT OF CASH AND FAILURE IN BUSINESS.

THE MOUTH

I. To dream that our mouth has grown larger means greater wealth in the house.

II. To dream that one's mouth is closed tightly and cannot be opened is a sign of approaching illness.

III. A bad taste in the mouth and a bad odor may signify falling into general contempt and being hated by one's servants.

THE CHEEKS

I. To have plump and vermilion cheeks is a good sign in dream. It means prosperity in business things and in the general sense.

II. To dream that one's cheeks are thin and pallid has the opposite significance.

To Ensure Your Dreams be True

It is advised that one should sleep in a pigsty; but one must sleep only on the back or on the face, and never on the side. One who does this as instructed is said to be assured of prophetic dreams.

To Dream of Foreign Lands

If one would dream of travels to strange places and distant countries, it is advised one feed upon a salad of French beans, cabbage, onions, broad beans, chestnuts and smallage before retiring, and these herbs shall provoke such visions.

A Means to Make a Man Sleep Sweetly

That we may have as great joy sleeping as waking, when we sup before we sleep, if we eat moderately of hind's tongue, balm and the like, when we sleep we shall have many fine conceits in dreams, that a man could not

DESIRE TO BE MORE MERRY AND TO SEE MORE
PLEASING THINGS, AS FIELDS, GARDENS, TREES,
FLOWERS, WE SHALL SEE SHADY DARK PLACES
COVERED WITH GREEN GRASS, AND CASTING OUT
EYES ABOVE, THE WHOLE WORLD SPRINGS UP AND
LOOKS VERY PLEASANTLY.

To See Visions by
The Magic Crystal

The Magic Crystal is a ball of pure virgin glass, somewhat in the shape of an egg. The method whereby one shall use it, is to first place yourself in a quiet room wherein you shall be entirely undisturbed, and taking care that the place be free from mirrors, ornaments, pictures, glaring colors, and so on which might otherwise distract attention. Hold the crystal in the palm of the right hand, and you shall retain it there from eleven to twelve o'clock at night, with the room dark, all the time concentrating your thoughts upon the object you desire to see with a steady, calm gaze. About twelve o'clock, the crystal becomes quite hot. Now look steadily into it, and you shall see pictures of scenes that appear are transpiring with friends far distant; in fact, it is asserted that the movements of any one can be known, whether husband, wife, lover or friend. And if you seek to know the future,

YOU SHALL MOST LIKELY BE IMPRESSED WITH KNOWLEDGE AS TO THE TIME AT WHICH THE EVENTS SHALL COME TO PASS, BUT IT MAY BE REGARDED THAT IN GENERAL VISIONS WHICH APPEAR IN THE EXTREME BACKGROUND INDICATE TIME MORE REMOTE, EITHER PAST OR FUTURE, THAN THOSE PERCEIVED NEARER AT HAND, AND THOSE WHICH SEEM MORE NEAR DENOTE THE PRESENT OR THE IMMEDIATE FUTURE. AND IF YOU WILL MAKE A QUERY ALOUD TO THE CRYSTAL, IT SHALL ANSWER IN THE AFFIRMATIVE BY WAY OF RISING CLOUDS, AND IF THE ANSWER TO YOUR QUESTION SHOULD BE NO, IT SHALL APPEAR BY WAY OF SINKING CLOUDS. AND YOU MAY ALSO KNOW THROUGH WHAT COLORS ARE SHOWN SOME DETAILS OF YOUR SUBJECT. WHITE CLOUDS OR COLORS ARE SUGGESTIVE OF GOOD AND OF FAVOR; BLACK SHALL INDICATE SORROW AND MISFORTUNES; RED OR YELLOW OR ORANGE PRESENT DANGER, SICKNESS, TROUBLE, GRIEF, DECEPTION, LOSS AND OTHER WOES; AND GREEN OR BLUE OR VIOLET MEAN JOY AND SUCCESS.

AND YOU MUST BE CAUTIOUS THAT NO OTHER PERSON EVER TOUCH YOUR CRYSTAL, UNLESS IT BE A

PERSON FOR WHOM YOU ARE INQUIRING, IN WHICH CASE THIS ONE MAY TOUCH IT FOR A FEW MOMENTS BEFORE YOUR USE; AND IF HE WOULD ATTEND YOU AS YOU LOOK INTO THE CRYSTAL HE MUST DO SO IN UTTER SILENCE AND KEEP HIMSELF AT A DISTANCE FROM YOU.

TWO PRINCIPAL CLASSES OF VISIONS WILL PRESENT THEMSELVES TO ONE USING THE CRYSTAL, THESE BEING THE SYMBOLIC AND THE ACTUAL VISIONS. SYMBOLIC VISIONS ARE THOSE THAT APPEAR AS SYMBOLS WHICH REPRESENT OTHER MEANINGS, WHILST THE ACTUAL VISIONS ARE PORTRAYALS OF SCENES AND EVENTS AS THEY TRULY EXIST, BE THEY MOVING OR OTHERWISE.

Divination by Oil

Some pour water into a glass basin, mixing therewith a drop of oil, and so think they see marvelous things in the water. It runneth thus, step by step:

I. Take the flask with oil, a small one, make with it thrice the sign of the cross on the head and face, saying

> IN THE NAME OF HEAVEN,
> OF THE STARS AND MOON,
> I PASS AWAY THIS TROUBLE
> FOR BETTER LUCK, AND SOON

II. With the same bottle or vial, make three crosses with the right hand over the glass of water, exactly from side to side, also making the corna or jettatura with the forefinger and little finger of the left hand extended, and the middle and ring-finger closed, or held by the thumb. And these extended fingers rest on the edge of the tumbler. While doing this you shall repeat:

BEFANIA BEFANIA BEFANIA
THOU WHO DIDST CAUSE THIS TROUBLE,
BEAR IT AWAY FROM ME

III. POUR IN OR LET FALL, VERY CAREFULLY, THREE DROPS OF OIL. IF THEY COMBINE AT ONCE, IT IS A GOOD SIGN, OR AN AFFIRMATIVE TO ANY QUESTION. IF YOU WISH TO KNOW WHETHER YOU ARE TO FIND WHAT YOU SEEK, OR MEET A FRIEND, OR ANYTHING OF THE KIND, ALL WILL GO AS YOU DESIRE. BUT IF THE THREE DROPS REMAIN APART IT IS A BAD OR NEGATIVE SIGN.

IV. THEN TO THOROUGHLY EXPLORE ALL THE CHANCES, THIS CEREMONY IS RENEWED THREE TIMES. AND EVERY TIME THROW THE WATER AND OIL INTO THE STREET, OR A COURT. SHOULD A MAN BE THE FIRST TO PASS, ALL WILL YET GO WELL. IF A WOMAN, THE OMENS ARE STILL UNFAVORABLE. AND THEN ONCE MORE MAKE THE CASTAGNA OR CHESTNUT, THE SIGN OF THE THUMB BETWEEN THE FORE AND MIDDLE FINGERS, WHICH IS FAR MORE POTENT THAN THE CORNA (EVEN THE EARLY ROMAN WRITERS CALL IT TERRIBLE) AND NOTE THAT THIS ALSO IS ON THE EDGE OF THE GLASS, WITH THE LEFT HAND, WHILE WITH THE RIGHT THE OIL IS DROPPED

SKILLFULLY SO AS TO MAKE A CROSS OF OIL, OR SPOTS OF OIL ACROSS THE WATER (WHICH HAS BEEN RENEWED). THEN CROSS THE HEAD AND FACE THREE TIMES WITH THE OIL, REPEATING THE BEFANIA INVOCATION THREE TIMES AS BEFORE.

V. AND IF, AFTER ALL, THE ORACLE IS UNPROPITIOUS, DROP INTO THE GLASS ABOUT A TEASPOONFUL OF SALT, AND REPEAT THE FORMULA OF BEFANIA. SHOULD THE OIL TURN OF A WHITISH COLOR, THIS IS A SIGN THAT THE BEFANIA RELENTS AND THAT ALL MAY YET GO WELL. BUT IF SHE BE DEAF TO EVERY SPELL, NOR HEED THE SACRED SALT, THEN DROP INTO THE GLASS A HOT COAL. THIS MIXES THE OIL AND WATER DESPITE OF ALL THE DEVILS. AND THIS DONE YOU GO FORTH WITH THE FIERCE, PROUD FEELING THAT THOUGH EVERY OMEN IS AGAINST YOU, YOU ARE TO PREVAIL BY A STRONG WILL.

VI. BUT ERE DEPARTING THERE IS STILL SOMETHING TO BE DONE. YOU EXPRESS YOUR GRATITUDE TO THE SPIRIT OF THE FIRE, WHICH IS SHORT BUT EXTREMELY HEATHEN, AND I HAVE NO DOUBT VERY ANCIENT:

O BLESSED FIRE,
THOU WHO BURNEST SO IMMENSELY,
THOU WHO WARMEST ALL MANKIND,

I PRAY THEE TO BURN THIS EVIL SPELL,
AND THE ONE WHO SMOTE ME WITH IT!

THEN, AS IN OLD LATIN RITES, THE COAL AND ALL MUST BE THROWN INTO A RUNNING STREAM, AND YOU DEPART WITHOUT LOOKING BEHIND YOU.

An Incense Whereby You May Divine

He that will foretell things was wont to have a fume applied to stir up his phantasie, which fumes being agreeable to certain spirits fit us to receive divine inspirations: So some say that a fume of linseed and fleaseed, with the roots of smallage and of violets, will make men see future things, and is good for divination.

To Know Your Future with Incense

Some call this Pyromantia, whereby powdered gums be thrown into the flames. If the flame rises in one, it is a good sign; if lambent and divided, unfortunate; if in three points, a glorious eventum or result; if much dispersed, an ill death; if crackling or snapping, misfortune; if it is very suddenly extinguished, great danger.

The Playing Cards
and their meanings

HEARTS

INDICATE AFFECTION AND CONTENTMENT.

KING.—A GOOD-HEARTED, EMOTIONAL PERSON; MELANCHOLY AND FRUSTRATION.

QUEEN.—A LOVING AND LOVABLE PERSON; DEVOTION.

JACK.—A WELL-LIKED PERSON, AS A FRIEND OR RELATIVE; ADMIRATION AND RESPECT.

TEN.—AMUSEMENT.

NINE.—THE WISH CARD. IT IS THE SIGN OF HAPPINESS AND SUCCESS.

EIGHT.—MATERIAL GOODS; ALSO, FRIENDLINESS.

SEVEN.—LOVESICKNESS AND SIMILAR DISTRESS.

SIX.—UNEXPECTED GOOD LUCK.

FIVE.—JEALOUSY AND ENVY.

FOUR.—A FORTUNATE CHANGE OF POSITION.

THREE.—A LACK OF PRUDENCE AND TACT.

TWO.—A WARM PARTNERSHIP.

ACE.—AN INTRODUCTION.

DIAMONDS

INDICATE FINANCIAL CONCERNS.

KING.—A SUCCESSFUL OR WEALTHY PERSON; SUCCESS OR WEALTH.

QUEEN.—A GOLD-DIGGER; GREED OR FLIRTATION.

JACK.—A FICKLE PERSON; A MATTER THAT SHOULD NOT BE RELIED UPON.

TEN.—PROSPERITY AND FULFILLMENT.

NINE.—BUSINESS.

EIGHT.—MATERIAL GOODS.

SEVEN.—GOSSIP, SCANDAL, OR ARGUMENTS.

SIX.—PROBLEMS.

FIVE.—UNEXPECTED BUT GENERALLY GOOD NEWS.

FOUR.—FINE LIVING.

THREE.—RENOWN, NOT NECESSARILY POSITIVE.

TWO.—NEGOTIATIONS.

ACE.—PROSPECTS.

CLUBS

INDICATE HARD WORK AND COMPETITION.

KING.—A HIGH-MINDED, HONEST PERSON; WISDOM AND VIRTUE.

QUEEN.—AN INTELLIGENT, UNDERSTANDING PERSON; CONFIDENCE AND HELP.

JACK.—A GENEROUS, TRUSTY FRIEND; A SURE AND DEPENDABLE MATTER.

TEN.—TRAVEL.

NINE.—GAIN AND ACHIEVEMENT.

EIGHT.—CONFUSION AND CONTENTION.

SEVEN.—STAGNATION.

SIX.—INVESTMENT OR LOSS OF MONEY.

FIVE.—NEW THINGS OR PEOPLE.

FOUR.—A WARNING AGAINST FALSEHOOD AND DOUBLE-DEALING.

THREE.—DISTRACTION.

TWO.—DISAPPOINTMENT.

ACE.—GOOD NEWS.

SPADES

INDICATE UNHAPPINESS AND STRIFE.

KING.—AN AMBITIOUS AND ILL-TEMPERED PERSON; WRATH.

QUEEN.—A SAD, UNSCRUPULOUS PERSON; DESPERATION.

JACK.—A WELL-MEANING, LAZY PERSON; SHIFTLESSNESS.

TEN.—ABANDONMENT.

NINE.—TROUBLE; ILLNESS, ESPECIALLY MENTAL.

Eight.—Greed.

Seven.—Sorrow and loss.

Six.—Small changes; a minor stroke of luck.

Five.—Interference.

Four.—Misfortune, but not lasting.

Three.—A journey.

Two.—Struggle.

Ace.—A terrible tragedy.

TO KNOW YOUR FORTUNE WITH CARDS

You shall take a deck of the cards, and shuffle the whole pack three times. You will remove the topmost card, and it shall provide you the answer you desire.

The Chaunse of the Dyce
being the old method whereby you may know your future from three dice

First be aware that my wisdom is poor,
If you are to be one who so comprehends
How to utilize dice to know Fortuna's store;
And doing a favor to entertain friends
Is all that your poor, silly author intends.
The way of the world, I have heard it said rife,
Is that men cannot all make the same feats in life.
I pray true to God that each fellow may cast
Using these, the three dice, what is true to his soul,
Whether he should be faithless, or whether steadfast,
So let it that grief or content be his dole
And allow that the wicked make goodness their goal.
Let those who have taken the trouble to throw
Find their fortunes should fall in the manner they know.
But do not attempt to hold me to account:
For Fortuna really is ruler of all,
So don't blame or thank me in any amount
Since I'm not the person who's making the call.
All I say for myself by my own wherewithal,
Is that never will trusting in Fate steer you wrong,
So I hope you'll enjoy, and she'll help you along.

EXPLIAT BALADE UPON THE CHAUNSE OF THE DYSE

666

JUST AS THE CLAMSHELL GIVES GROWTH TO THE PEARL,
TO EVERY GOOD VIRTUE YOU ARE THE DEVICE.
YOUR CHASTITY'S CLEAN AND UNTAINTED AS BERYL;
AS CINNAMON'S ODOR, SO SWEET AND SO NICE;
YOUR MEEKNESS PRESERVES YOU AGAINST EVERY VICE.
FOR THOSE WHO ARE CLEARLY AWARE OF YOUR MERIT,
THEY FIND THERE IS NOTHING WITH WHICH TO COMPARE IT.

665

TO ENTERTAIN THOUGHTS OF SO AWFUL A CAD
IS SHAMEFUL TO SUCH A DEGREE, I COULD QUIT.
THE FACT IS I HAVEN'T WORDS IN ME SO BAD
AS ARE NEEDED TO CHIDE YOU; MY TONGUE IS NOT FIT;
AND YET YOUR SUCCESSES IN LOVE STUMP THE WIT.
WHERE JASON CHEATS ONE YOU ARE CHEATING ON TWO,
AND BY GOD, I HOPE NOT TO LEARN MORE OF YOU.

664

FOR SUCH A GOOD CHEER YOU'RE HELD HIGH IN REPUTE,
AND EVERYONE KNOWS YOU'RE SO LOYAL AND TRUE

THAT ALL THOSE WHO'D SEEK TO YIELD SUCH VIRTUE'S FRUIT,
AS A WAY TO PASS TIME AND HAVE SOMETHING TO DO,
ARE SAD IF YOU'VE OTHERS AHEAD IN YOUR QUEUE.
THE MERITS THAT YOU, ON THESE PEOPLE, CAN PRESS,
PROTECT AND PRESERVE YOU FROM ALL FOOLISHNESS.

663
SO FIERCELY AND CONFIDENTLY DID YOU CAST,
AND YET IT'S NO WONDER: YOU'RE SO OVERBOLD.
WITH STUPID AND SAUCY FOLK SHOULD YOU BE CLASSED,
AND YET, WITH SUCH CUNNING ARE WORDS YOU SPEAK ROLLED,
THAT NEVER SHOULD ANYONE TRUST WHAT YOU'VE TOLD;
BUT IF EVER FOLKS SEE YOU JUMP OUT AND DANCE,
YOU'RE NEVER CONCERNED ABOUT HOW WELL YOU PRANCE.

662
ALTHOUGH YOU ARE HARDLY THE FAIREST OF ALL,
YOU'VE KINDLY, GOOD WAYS AND ARE NATURALLY CARING.
FOR YOU, EVERYONE MAKES EXCUSES TO CALL,
AND CONSTANTLY SEEKS THAT THEY BE WITH YOU, PAIRING,
BECAUSE THEY ARE SO WELL IMPRESSED WITH YOUR BEARING.
WHOMEVER THE FORTUNATE FRIEND YOU WILL SEE,
YOUR GOODLINESS GLADDENS TO HIGHEST DEGREE.

661

YOU HOLD YOUR HEAD HIGH IN AN ARROGANT MOOD;
THE WEATHERCOCK SOONER WOULD FLY THAN YOU'D KILL
OFF YOUR EATING WHEN HAPS YOU'RE PRESENTED WITH FOOD.
YOUR STOMACH SWELLS UP TILL IT LOOKS LIKE YOU WILL
VERY SHORTLY GIVE BIRTH TO THE SHAFT OF CORNHILL,
THEN GOD JOSTLES YOU (SO TO PUNISH, NO QUESTION)
THAT THE STREET RIGHTLY ECHOES WITH YOUR INDIGESTION.

655

YOU THINK THAT YOUR FUTURE IS SETTLED IN PLACE,
THAT THE FORTUNE YOU'RE READING IS TRUE AND PRECISE;
AND ANY TIME OTHERS AND YOU SHARE A SPACE,
YOU EVER ARE TRYING TO GIVE THEM ADVICE
FOR, COMES IT TO COUNCIL, YOU'RE QUITE THE DEVICE,
SINCE ALL THAT YOU'RE TOLD, YOU BELIEVE EVERY WORD,
AND FEEL, THEREFORE, EQUALLY YOU SHOULD BE HEARD.

654

WERE IT NOT THAT THE PARTIES YOU THROW ARE THE BEST
NOBODY EVER WOULD BOTHER TO GO:
THE WEALTH AND THE OPULENCE SHOWN AT YOUR FEST
IS BETTER BELOVED THAN THE ACTIONS YOU SHOW,
BECAUSE YOU HAVE MANNERS AS BAD AS I KNOW.

PLEASE TROUBLE TO GET YOUR PHYSIOGNOMY DONE,
AND DON'T LOOK SO STARTLED; MY LIES HAVE BEEN NONE.

653

MERCURY, GIVING YOU FORCE OF FAIR SPEECH,
WAS CAUGHT AT ATTENTION WHEN YOUR BIRTH DID FALL,
AND FIXED IT THAT STUDY AND SKILL WERE IN REACH.
SURPASSING THE SKILL AND THE KNOWLEDGE OF ALL,
AND OTHER THINGS TOO THAT YOU'LL LATER RECALL,
YOU UTILIZE WORDS WITH SUCH CAUTION AND CARE
THAT ANYONE FEELS HIMSELF FLATTERED AND FAIR.

652

WITHOUT BEING THOUGHTFUL OR HOLDING THINGS BACK,
YOU SAY LOUD AND BOISTEROUS JUST WHAT YOU THINK; ALL:
AND SO WELL-DETERMINED'S THE NOTION YOU PACK,
THAT ONCE IT'S BEEN SAID, YOU'D REPEAT THE FULL CALL
AND TO DRIVE THE POINT HOME YOU WOULD TEAR
                                    THROUGH THE WALL.
NOBODY BACKS YOU: YOU'RE LEADER TO NONE.
YOUR BRAIN'S OF A SORT AT WHICH FOOLS WOULD POKE FUN.

651

Your constance won't waiver, you're steady of heart,
Your actions display you as faithful and true,
And doubleness has in you no single part.
You hold your heart open and shun all defense,
Your passion drives forward the love that you sense,
But were it your lover should motion to fly,
I then would advise, you should let your faith die.

644

I advise everybody be cautious with you:
Your dishonest nature is one that you mask,
You're skilled to make people know not what they do.
None, by your looks, for acquaintance should ask,
But at least you have courage that's up to the task.
Like leaves in the wind, you race forward most deft,
And feeling no fear for the life you leave left.

643

Truly it's stated that you've been well wrought,
For anyone able to read of your fate
Will not find there wickedness, nor idle thought.
God loves you so much, that his own joy to sate,
He fully ensured that you should become great.

YES, THERE IS NOT LIFE WITHIN THIS PLANET'S SPACE
AS I THINK COULD BE SETTLED MORE HIGH IN HIS GRACE.

642
HELLO AGAIN, WELCOME! WHAT'S KEPT YOU SO, CUTIE?
WE'VE WAITED ON YOU AND WE'RE HAPPY TO SEE
THAT WHILE WE WERE DANCING YOU STUCK TO YOUR DUTY,
AND SAT ON THE TOILET, TO STRIVE SERIOUSLY
ENSURING YOU MASTER YOUR IDIOCY.
IF ANY MAN MATCHED YOU IN MEMORIZED WIT,
HE BOUGHT IT TOO DEAR PAID HE ONE GROAT FOR IT.

641
O VISION OF ULTIMATE HUMBLENESS MET
AMONGST ANY CREATURE THAT'S FOUND HERE ON EARTH.
IN THIS PERSON, WISDOM AND SKILL HAVE BEEN SET,
OF THIS I CAN PROMISE, MY WORDS DO HOLD WORTH.
MAY GOD GRANT MUCH VIRTUE, OF VICE GIVE A DEARTH,
PERFECTION OF BEAUTY WITHOUT ENVY'S STARES
AND LET YOU BE FAITHFUL WITHOUT JEALOUS CARES.

633
A PERSON LIKE YOU, O, WHERE'D FIND I ANOTHER,
THAT COULD ACT IN SO WICKED A MANNER AS YOU

On God's own green earth, from one end to the other?
No one could shill off an item less true,
Than that which will spill from your mouth sees you do.
You're leading your life while you're lying so loud,
So you can conceal your deceit in a cloud.

632
There is no such thing as can gladden my heart,
Nor which from depression can draw me away
Regardless what's happened or what pain I smart,
More than your fair singing, heard whene'er I may,
With such pleasant voice that I'm daring to say
That never was anyone brought greater joy
Since the moment Criseyde met with Troilus in Troy.

631
Tip of the hat, for you've cast your dice well.
You always come slowly, with patience sublime,
While on your face, such serious looks there do dwell,
Yet I can't find words, not with prose nor with rhyme,
Even though I could write night till noontime
Describing your gluttony, and your great sloth;
Yes really, you are one pestiferous moth.

622

IF MATCHING YOUR APTITUDE WERE TO BE TRIED,
PEOPLE WOULD BENEFIT FROM SUCH A STAKE.
EVERYONE WISHES TO BE BY YOUR SIDE,
AND ALL THAT'S ENDEAVORED THAT YOU UNDERTAKE
IS BETTERED BY WHATEVER EFFORTS YOU MAKE.
YOUR SKILL I WOULD WISH I COULD SO MUCH AS GLANCE;
SUCH WORTHINESS I'D USE TO GREATLY ADVANCE.

621

GOOD GOD, STAND ABACK! FOR SHAME, WHY CAST YOU SO?
WAS REALLY THIS FORTUNE THE ONLY YOU FOUND,
FROM ALL OF THESE CHANCES BEFORE YOU THAT SHOW,
THOUGH SO MANY OTHERS COULD BE HAD MORE SOUND?
WELL, DESTINY FINDS HERE YOUR PENANCE TAKES GROUND:
FOR NO ONE MAKES BETTER A PIMP OR A LOUT
ANYWHERE HERE IN THE WHOLE LAND ABOUT.

611

NOW DON'T SHY AWAY UNTIL YOU'VE HAD YOUR CHANCE.
ALTHOUGH, FROM YOUR YOUTH, YOU'RE NOT CUNNING OF MIND,
YOUR GOODNESS SHALL YET ENSURE YOU SHALL ADVANCE
TO ESCAPE THE DESIRE WHICH YOUR HEART DOES BIND;
YOUR NAME WILL BE WORSHIPPED ONE DAY, YOU WILL FIND,

AND FINALLY FULL WELL YOU SHALL SURELY ATTAIN
THE JOY WHERETOFORE YOU'VE BEEN LIVING IN PAIN.

555
YOU'VE JUST HIT THE JACKPOT, IN THIS GAME YOU PLAYED,
SO HANG ON A SECOND AND LEARN WHAT YOU'VE WON:
YOUR EQUAL IN BOASTING HAS NEVER BEEN MADE
AMONGST ANY PERSON WHO WALKS 'NEATH THE SUN,
SO HERE'S HOW THE WHEEL OF FORTUNE HAS RUN:
YOU'LL PUT ON A WHETSTONE AS MARK OF YOUR LYING
EVEN WHILE ALL OF THE COUNTRY'S ESPYING.

554
YOU ACT WELL FOR YOUR AGE, FOR THAT LET US GOD PRAISE;
YOU'VE SPENT YOUR YOUTH SUCH THAT THERE'S NOTHING TO BLAME,
WITH A HEART THAT'S GROWN FAMOUS, AND CAUTIONOUS WAYS,
AND SURELY I WISH THAT NOW SUCH A CROWD CAME.
TO ANYONE FINDING THEY'RE CRAVING SUCH FAME:
YOU'VE WITNESSED SO MUCH, AND SO MUCH OF IT HOLD,
THAT YOU COULD WELL TEACH IT TO BOTH YOUNG AND OLD.

553
WHEN IT COMES TO THIS CAST, NO ONE ELSE FITS THE BILL,
SO CERTAINLY YOU BROUGHT YOURSELF TO ITS SAY.

YOU TAKE NO REGARD WHEN THE WORLD THINKS YOU ILL;

THE CLOCK WILL STRIKE TWELVE ONLY TWICE IN A DAY,

AND YET AT EACH TIME YOU CHANGE THOUGHTS SOME NEW WAY.

IN LOVE YOU DO NOT ACHIEVE VENIAL SIN,

SO AT LEAST IN THAT FORTUNE YOU'RE ABLE TO WIN.

552

O GODDESS, O NATURE, IT'S YOU I ADDRESS.

I HOPE YOU WERE MOST HIGHLY PLEASED IN THAT HOUR

AT WHICH YOU THIS MOST WONDERFUL CREATURE DID PRESS,

WHOM, OUT OF ALL BEAUTY, IS CHIEF HIGHEST TOWER,

WITH WHOM SO MAY VIRTUE FIND SUCCOR AND POWER.

HE THAT WOULD SEEK TO HAVE SOMETHING FROM YOU

WOULD FIND IN THE EFFORT YOUR GRACE THROUGH

AND THROUGH.

551

YOU KEEP YOURSELF BUSY —FIE UPON IDLENESS!

DESPITE THAT NO PERSON COMPLETES SOON AS STARTED

WHEN IT COMES TO NEW PROJECTS, THAT'S YET WHAT YOU STRESS.

PERHAPS THEN SOME HELP TO YOU MAY BE IMPARTED:

THE CURE IS SOON COMING, I SAY SO FULL-HEARTED;

A PERSON FROM TRAVELS RETURNING BACK HOME

MAY FIND SUDDEN CHANCE IN HIS LIFE MIGHT SOON ROAM.

544

WITH YOU VICE HAS FOUND ITSELF TOTALLY BLOCKED
SINCE YOU SO DESIRE TO FIGHT IT COMPLETE,
IN YOU FINDS THE CALM OF GRISELDA RESTOCKED.
SO SAY MEN OF YOU THAT ONE WON'T BETTER MEET,
AND WITH NONE MORE WELL COULD ONE LET THEIR TRUST SEAT;
THEREBY HAS VIRTUE SO FURTHERED YOUR NAME,
THAT WELL IT IS KNOWN LACKING MALICE OR BLAME.

543

YOU CAST THE DICE COLD FROM YOUR HAND, IT IS CLEAR,
AND I AM IN WONDER THAT SUCH COULD BE TRUE
BECAUSE I HAVE HEARD YOU HAVE NO SHAME OR FEAR
TO PERFORM AN ILL ACTION; BUT LAZINESS TOO,
I AM SORRY TO SAY, IS A GREAT SKILL YOU DO;
LIKE SHOOTING A SAUSAGE BY CROSSBOW YOU FLY.
LORD, WOE TO THE MAN WHO ON YOU MUST RELY.

542

WE WELCOME YOUR PRESENCE, FOR REALLY, GREAT JOY
IS BROUGHT TO US THANKS TO YOUR VISITING HERE,
FOR ANYPLACE OUT IN THE TOWN OF NEW TROY
THERE'S NONE WHO AT DANCING OR GLEE CAN COME NEAR.

SUCH MEN AS WILL LISTEN TO YOU, WELL MAY HEAR
YOUR KNOWLEDGEFUL SPEECH OF THE GOD OF LOVE'S TEACHING,
BUT THAT IS YOUR DOWNFALL; HAVE DONE WITH THE PREACHING.

541
YOU'RE AS PRETTY A NOTE AT THIS TIME AS IS KNOWN,
AND ALWAYS LOOK CHEERED WHEN YOU HERE AND THERE WEND.
YOUR MAKE WAS NOT FASHIONED FROM FLESH NOR FROM BONE.
A NOBLE PROTECTOR AND MOST GENTLE FRIEND
YOU MAKE WHEN TO GIRLS YOUR COMPANIONSHIP LEND,
AS FELLOWS IN ARTHUR'S TIME WERE WONT TO TAKE
TO COURT WITH THEM ALL OUT OF COUPLING'S SAKE.

533
GOD KNOWS YOU ARE ABLE AT ALL THAT YOU DO,
FREE FROM ALL ENVY OR INSTINCT FOR SPITING;
ALL THAT YOUR BRAIN WOULD BE LET TO IMBUE,
WHETHER IT'S CLERGY OR WHETHER IT'S WRITING
OR HUNTING OR HAWKING OR KNIGHTHOOD OR FIGHTING,
YOU'VE LEARNED IT AS SO TO HAVE GREAT UNDERSTANDING,
THAT NO ONE FOR FURTHER WIT COULD BE DEMANDING.

532

ON THE SUBJECT OF MANNERS, YOU KNOW QUITE A LOT:
PROBABLY LEARNED IN THE OUTSKIRTS OF TOWN.
WHENEVER YOUR QUARRELS ARE FORCED TO BE FOUGHT,
WITH YOUR BACK TO THE WALL YOU REFUSE TO BACK DOWN,
AND FOR COURTESY TOSS YOU OUT ALL YOUR RENOWN.
YOU ONLY CAN LEARN BY THE PUNCHES ONE THROWS,
EVEN THOUGH THAT'S JUST WHAT BRINGS YOU TO BLOWS.

531

YOUR HOME IS NOT HERE AND FOR THAT BE YOU PROUD.
GO QUICK, FOR OPPONENTS OF YOURS DWELL IN HERE!
THERE CAN PROTECTION YOUR MEEKNESS ENSHROUD,
AND VICE FROM THE BODY CAN ALL BE PUT CLEAR,
EVEN THOUGH NO ONE CAN DRIVE IT OR STEER;
ONLY YOUR CHARITY SELFLESSLY MOVES:
YOUR NICKNAME THE PRINCESS OF VIRTUE SO PROVES.

522

WE WERE STARTING TO THINK YOU HAD GOT INTO TROUBLE.
WHERE HAVE YOU TARRIED SO LONG BY AND BY?
YOU'RE BLUSHING; O STOP THAT, STOP NOW, ON THE DOUBLE!
AND TRY TO EXTINGUISH THAT SPARK IN YOUR EYE,
YOUR FORTUNE IS READY FOR YOU TO ESPY:

THE IMAGE THE OUTFIT YOU WEAR DOES ENDOW
SUCH FAIRNESS AS WOULD DO A SADDLE A COW.

521
ALAS, HOW YOU DARE TO TURN UP IN THESE PARTS!
SO WOULD I TO GOD YOU WERE BANISHED FROM HERE,
FOR PLAINLY YOU TOY WITH AND SHATTER TRUE HEARTS.
INTO MEN'S LIVES SUCH BAD PROBLEMS YOU REAR,
THAT, LACKING PROTECTION, THEY COWER IN FEAR.
I KNOW OF YOUR LOVE AND THE TRICKS OF YOUR ART,
FOR I HAVE MYSELF FELT THOSE PANGS IN MY HEART.

511
FOLKS WHO ARE LIKE YOU ARE FEW TO BE FOUND,
AND WOE UNTO US WHEN YOUR LIFE SHOULD EXHAUST,
FOR ONCE IT SHOULD PASS THAT YOU'RE LAID IN THE GROUND,
FREE GOODNESS IS LOCKED UP, THE KEY TO IT LOST.
ONE WHO WITH YOU HIS REQUEST SHOULD ACCOST,
YOU'RE HAPPY TO GRANT IT WITH UTMOST OF SPEED,
SO IGNORANT ARE YOU OF EVIL AND GREED.

444
LUCK TO THE MAN THAT YOUR FAVORS DESERVE,
AND LITTLE MORE ON YOU NEED BE UNDERSTOOD.

No match to your skill's so well able to serve;
Your tongue never stops in the speaking of good.
Would that more folks who could act that way would!
And any such person with whom you'd consort
Is glad for it, thanks to your kindly comport.

443
My wit is not adequate as to declare
Your leadership skills and your merits genteel.
Your jubilant worry and joyful despair
You're able, most truly, quite well to conceal
From any with whom you are gaming, you feel.
While lovers are rising to join in a dance,
You take an ill-tempered and warrior-like stance.

442
Worshipful Mars, O so mighty in war:
All that is battle is in your control
And follows what wishes you have in your store,
And so it proceeds to conclude to its whole.
You've certainly settled your pleasure to dole
Reward to this most noble creature from you,
So much that he never finds strife in his view.

441

When it comes to old stories, you give them great heed.
Too bad your collection of books was not vast,
For really you're skillful at going to read:
The Wife of Bath's tale you've learned first to last.
The man may well say that too swift and too fast
Did he choose, who would find himself wedded with you.
And yet with no wife surely he'd be the shrew.

433

The men that could praise you are too long to list.
You're known for how pious and careful you guard,
And this fame grows such it will never desist,
So many record how at good you work hard.
Would that I, as you could, act with such true regard,
And so well could act, from beginning to end,
As you at the things your attention should lend.

432

At such rare events where you might hold your tongue,
Your insides might burst, in you envy so flies,
And starts it to think, without care how it sprung:
"My power of speech to me no one denies,
So shut up this fellow, or I'll see he dies!"

AND SOON OF THE SUCKER WHO'S TAKING YOUR TIME
YOU FIND THAT YOU FEEL HIS MURDER'S NO CRIME.

431
YOU'RE WORTHY INDEED TO FIND LUCK SHOULD BEFALL,
AND SO YOU SHALL HAVE IT AS MUCH AS DESERVED,
FOR NEVER I KNEW ANY PERSON AT ALL
COULD BETTER BE THOUGHT AS MAN OF HIS WORD;
SO TRUSTING IN YOU, LET ALL MEN BE ASSURED
THAT ALL HIGHEST THOUGHTS THAT ONE'S ABLE TO GIVE
ARE DUE UNTO YOU WHERESOEVER YOU LIVE.

422
YOU BABBLE SO MUCH THAT NO PERSON SHOULD LET YOU;
BUT YOU WON'T ALLOW ANY OTHERS THEIR SAY.
THEY BLOW FROM REPRESSION SO'S NOT TO UPSET YOU,
THOSE WHO HAVE FORTUNE SO ILL AS TO STAY,
WHICH THEY MUST; THEY'VE NO JUNCTURE TO SCUTTLE AWAY,
SO RASHLY YOU BABBLE WITH NO END IN SIGHT
AND LEAVING YOUR VICTIMS WITH NO MEANS TO FIGHT.

421
YOU'RE FLAWLESS WITH MUSIC, NO MAN CAN DENY.
IN FACT YOU'RE PERFECTION AT ANY FINE GAME,

BUT WHEN IT SO HAPPENS YOU WISTFULLY CRY,
SINGING SAD SONGS WITH A HARP AS YOUR FRAME,
THE MIXTURE OF BEAUTY AND SONG BRING YOU FAME,
AND YOU HAVE SUCH SKILL, FOR NO OTHER SO SINGS
IN THE WAY THAT YOU DO WHEN YOU'RE PLAYING THE STRINGS.

411

MY GOD, QUIT YOUR CROWDING, STOP PRESSING ME SO!
LET'S HURRY TO LET THIS ONE KNOW OF HIS CHANCE.
YOU'RE MAKING YOURSELF SUCH A NUISANCE, YOU KNOW,
AND DO SO ALL OVER, FROM SCOTLAND TO FRANCE,
BUT THAT IS EXPECTED; YOUR SKILL'S LIKE YOUR STANCE.
PHYSIOGNOMY DICTATES AS MUCH, SO YOU'RE BOUND
TO BE QUITE A LARGE BASTARD, AS BIG AS I'VE FOUND.

333

SINCERELY AND KINDLY, TO ACT AS A BUFFER,
MAY ANY MAN CRY OF HIS AWFUL DISTRESS.
ALAS AND ALACK! O WHY IS IT YOU SUFFER
WHEN PICTURES OF VIRTUE AND TRUTH YOU IMPRESS?
HOW IS IT FORTUNE'S NOT HEEDED YOUR STRESS,
AND DONE BY YOU RIGHTLY AS YOU SHOULD DESERVE,
SINCE COMFORT IS DUE FOR THE ACTIONS YOU SERVE?

332

A good job indeed, you're on point with your lot.
Your master is Sloth, and by you he's out-sinned.
Impressive that you should achieve what you sought:
You're as like to press forth as you are to be pinned,
But there's an old saying, or so I get wind:
"You can't make a silk purse from ear of a sow"
And such of you, all that have met you will vow.

331

No one condemns you your skill with direction;
Regarding foreknowledge, you're surely the master,
You're utterly brimming with wit in each section;
No other can see where the Fates will fall faster,
You know how to stave off most any disaster.
Such large store of wisdom in such a small space
I never dreamed able to form in one place.

322

You find something suspicious of all whom you see.
You're jealous, unfriendly and contrary, too.
Your arrogance rules you to such a degree
That if you should find a nice couple in view,
You wedge yourself in and force talk about you.

CATO THE WISE SAYS THAT THOSE WHO FIND FAULT
IN OTHERS, THEMSELVES HAVE NOT MUCH TO EXALT.

321

I'M LACKING THE SKILL I WOULD NEED TO DESCRIBE
YOUR GOVERNING SMARTNESS AND GREAT EXALTATION
THAT UNTO YOU TRULY SHOULD PEOPLE ASCRIBE:
HUMANITY'S SPRING-WELL AND ALL GOOD'S CAUSATION.
SO TRULY YOU'VE COME UPON FATE'S ALLOCATION;
YOU'RE SO MUCH BELOVED BY ALL THOSE WHO SHOULD FACE YOU
THAT NONE IN THIS WORLD COULD BE USED TO REPLACE YOU.

311

TRULY AS EVER, THE DICE SAY OF YOU:
CRISEYDE IN THE FLESH ARE, IN ACTION AND DEED.
I'M HOPING THAT HERE PEOPLE ALREADY KNOW
A PAINTER REDIPPING HIS BRUSH HAS NO NEED
TO DO SO AS OFT AS YOU PLANT LOVE'S NEW SEED;
BUT STILL YOU RANK HIGHLY IN MERCY AND GRACE,
ALTHOUGH YOU BE ROAMING ALL OVER THE PLACE.

222

O HOW COULD IT FALL YOU TOOK SO LONG TO FIND?
NOW LET'S GIVE THE READING YOUR CASTING DEMANDS:

Even a fellow who's functionally blind,
Who merely might feel the shape of your hands,
Will find yet your beauty he still understands.
He never could glean nor have means to fulfill
A circumstance better, that joy could instill.

221
Everyone's happy that's working for you,
And none of them ever incline to forget
Your leadership rendered so thoughtful and true,
Ensuring that everything needed is set;
And readily is it that your heart will let
Every man have what rewards are his due,
That leaving your service is last thing they'd do.

211
Mercy to God, there's no how, there's no when,
To know what you're thinking, it's not known by one:
For even if found you some thousands of men,
Of whom you could tease and aggrieve just for fun,
They yet would still feel that no harm was done,
By talking to them like you were their best friend,
Even though malice is all you intend.

111

AT LAST WE ARRIVE AT THE CLOSE OF OUR TALE.
UNLUCKY'S THE CAST BUT THE FORTUNE'S EXACT:
ALTHOUGH YOU HAVE DONE AS OBLIGED, WITHOUT FAIL,
YOUR VIRTUE DOES NOTHING TO HELP YOU, IN FACT.
I KNOW IT THE MORE BY MY OWN MEANS TO ACT,
FOR CHANCE NOW HAS GIVEN UP RULING ME SO,
AND THUS IT IS SADLY MY TIME NOW TO GO.

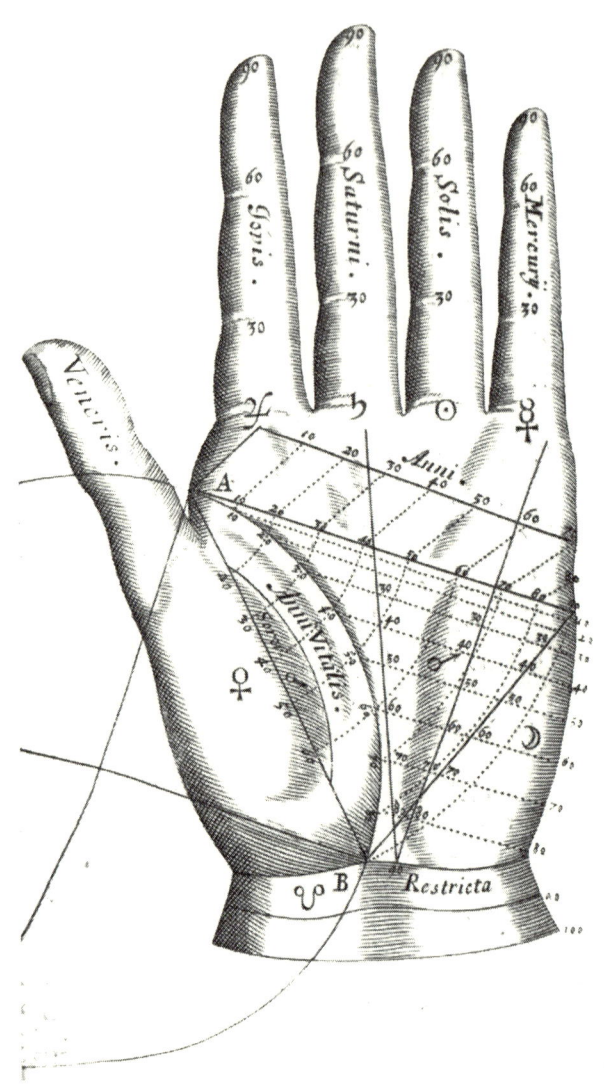

A Rational Demonstration of Chiromantical Signatures

The foundation of Chiromancy depends upon the true appropriation of the several mounts, fingers, or places in the hand to their proper stars or planets. The ancients have assigned the root of the middle-finger to Saturn, of the fore-finger to Jupiter; of the hollow of the hand to Mars: the root of the ring-finger to Sol: of the thumb to Venus: of the little-finger to Mercury, and lastly the brawn of the hand near the wrist to Luna. That line which comes round the ball of the thumb towards the root or mount of Jupiter is called Linea Jovialis or the life-line: that from the wrist to the root or mount of Saturn, Linea Saturnialis: but if it points to the root or mount of Sol, Linea Solaris, if to Mercury, Linea Mercurialis: that which goes from Linea Jovialis to the mount of Luna, Linea Lunaris, or the natural line: the other great line above it is called Linea Stellata, or the line of fortune, because it limits the mounts of the planets, and is impressed with

VARIOUS VENUES IN THOSE PLACES ACCORDING TO THE NATURE OF THE PLANET WHOSE MOUNT IT RUNS UNDER OR SETS A BOUNDARY UNTO LASTLY, THE SPACE BETWEEN THE NATURAL LINE AND THE LINE OF FORTUNE IS CALLED MENSA, THE TABLE. ALL OTHER LINES SHALL EITHER PROCEED OUT OF THE SIDES OF THE FORMER, OR ELSE FROM SOME PROPER MOUNT. EVERY LINE GREAT OR SMALL, LONG OR SHORT, HATH A CERTAIN BEGINNING OR ROOT, FROM WHICH IT RISES; AND A CERTAIN END OR POINT TO WHICH IT TENDS. THE DISTANCE BETWEEN BOTH ENDS, IS THE WAY OF ITS PASSAGE; IN WHICH WAY, IT EITHER CROSSES SOME OTHER LINE, OR ELSE IS CROSSED; IF IT DO NEITHER, ITS SIGNIFICATION IS CONTINUAL, AND OUGHT SO MUCH THE MORE TO BE TAKEN NOTICE OF. EVERY MOUNT HATH A PROPER SIGNIFICATION, WHICH IT RECEIVES FROM THE SIGNIFICATIONS OF ITS PROPER PLANET, BEING ABSTRACTLY CONSIDERED; THE SAME UNDERSTAND OF ALL THE PRINCIPAL LINES AFORESAID.

SATURN

THE AUTHOR OF AGE, INHERITANCES, MELANCHOLY, MALICE, SORROW, MISERY, CALAMITIES, ENEMIES, IMPRISONMENTS, SICKNESS, DISEASES, PERPLEXITIES, CARES, POVERTY, CROSSES, DEATH, AND, WHATSOEVER EVIL CAN BEFALL HUMAN LIFE: HE SIGNIFIES FATHERS, OLD MEN, LABORERS, DYERS, SMITHS, AND JESUITS. HE ALSO SIGNIFIES ONE AUSTERE AND SATIRICAL, WITH A HEAD DECLINING, EYES FIXED UPON THE EARTH, HANGING LIPS AND A SULLEN COUNTENANCE, WASTING HIMSELF WITH A FURIOUS SILENCE. HE GIVES A COMPLEXION OR COLOR BETWEEN BLACK AND YELLOW, MEAGER, DISTORTED, OF AN HARD SKIN, EMINENT VEINS, SMALL EYES; EYE-BROWS ALMOST JOINED TOGETHER, A THIN BEARD, THICK LIPS; CAST DOWN LOOKS, A HEAVY GAIT, AND STUMBLING AS HE GOES. HE SIGNIFIES ENVY, AND ENVIOUS MEN, A WAYLAYER OR PADDER UPON THE HIGHWAY. BUT WHERE HE IS WELL PLACED HE SIGNIFIES ONE SUBTLE, WISE, OR WITTY, INTELLIGENT, INGENIOUS, ONE OF PROFOUND THOUGHTS, GIVEN UP TO SECRET CONTEMPLATIONS, A PRESERVER, OR

KEEPER OF HIDDEN THINGS AND A FINDER OUT OF
THINGS THAT ARE LOST.

JUPITER

THE AUTHOR OF HEALTH, STRENGTH MODERATION, SOBRIETY, MERCY, RICHES, SUBSTANCE, GOODNESS, LIBERTY, RELIGION, HONESTY, JUSTICE, MODESTY, AND ALL OTHER THINGS WHICH MAY MAKE A MAN HAPPY: HE SIGNIFIES CHURCHES, CHURCH-MEN, LAWYERS, SCHOLARS, CLOTHIERS, AND THE LIKE. HE SIGNIFIES ONE GOOD NATURED, FORTUNATE, SWEET, PLEASANT, A WELL-WISHER; ONE HONEST, NEAT, OF GOOD PARENTAGE, AND HONORABLE. HE GIVES CHEERFULNESS, RIGHT JUDGMENT, TRUTH, HEAVENLY WISDOM, UNDERSTANDING, AND IS THE BESTOWER OF RICHES, GOODNESS AND VIRTUE. HE DENOTES ONE MERRY, INGENIOUS, FAIR, HONORABLE, HOSPITABLE, KIND, AND EVERY WAYS GOOD. HE PREFIGURES A MAN OF A SANGUINE COMPLEXION BETWEEN WHITE AND RED, OF A DELICATE BODY, GOOD STATURE, HIGH FOREHEAD, AND A HEAD LIFTED UP; EYES SOMEWHAT BIG, SHORT NOSTRILS, LARGE TEETH, A LIGHT COLORED BEARDS, A TALL COMPLETE BODY, HONEST, JUST AND FAIR CONDITIONED.

MARS

THE AUTHOR OF STRIFE, CONTENTION, PRIDE, PRESUMPTION, TYRANNY, THEFTS, MURDERS, VICTORY, CONQUEST, IMPORTUNACY, BOLDNESS AND DANGERS: HE SIGNIFIES PHYSICIANS, SURGEONS, APOTHECARIES, THE CAMP, ALL MILITARY MEN AND PREFERMENTS, EDGE-TOOLS, BUTCHERS, CARPENTERS, GUNNERS, BAILIFFS, AND THE LIKE. HE IS THE AUTHOR OF WAR, FIGHTING, BLOOD, AND STRIFE, AND SIGNIFIES ONE STRONGHOLD, QUARRELSOME, INSOLENT, A TRAITOR OR A SUBVERTER AND OVERTURNER OF STATES AND KINGDOMS. HE GIVES SOWER AND MIGHT, HEAT AND BURNING, AND SIGNIFIES VIOLENCE, CONTENTION, IMPUDENCE, AND ALL DISORDERED, INCONSIDERATE, AND HEADY ACTIONS. HIS COUNTENANCE IS TERRIBLE, CRUEL, FIERCE, ANGRY, PROUD, HASTY AND IMPERIOUS. HE GIVES A RED COMPLEXION, DEEP YELLOW OR BLACKS HAIR, ROUND VISAGE, FIERY EYES, AND A SAVAGE REVENGEFUL LOOK WELL PLACED, HE SIGNIFIES SURGEONS, CAPTAINS, COMMANDERS, AND GREAT MEN UNDER MILITARY DISCIPLINE.

SOL

THE AUTHOR OF HONOR, GLORY, RENOWN, PREFERMENT, LIFE, GENEROSITY, MAGNANIMITY, SOVEREIGNTY, DOMINION, POWER, TREASURES, GOLD, SILVER, AND WHATSOEVER MAY MAKE THE LIFE OF MAN SPLENDID; HE SIGNIFIES KINGS, PRINCES, RULERS, AND ALL MEN IN POWER; MINTERS, GOLD-SMITHS, LONG LIFE AND WISDOM. HE SIGNIFIES ONE OF A NOBLE AND GENEROUS NATURE, FORTUNE, HONEST, NEAT, PRUDENT, INTELLIGENT, WIFE, THE GOVERNOR AND BESTOWER OF LIFE AND BEAUTY, AND THE DISPELLER OF EVIL. HE GIVES COURAGE, HONOR AND MAJESTY, A MAN CONSIDERATE, WISE AND PRUDENT, ONE OF A MIDDLE STATURE, COMELY PERSONAGE, CURLED HAIR AND BROWNISH, OF A RED OR SANGUINE COMPLEXION, TRUSTY AND MAGNANIMOUS; BUT BEING ILL PLACED, VAINGLORIOUS AND A TYRANT.

VENUS

THE AUTHOR OF JOY, PLEASURE, MIRTH, SOLACE, LUST, UNCLEANNESS AND IDLENESS: SHE SIGNIFIES WOMAN-KIND, SISTERS, LADIES, WHORES, CURIOSITIES, LAPIDARIES, SILKMEN, TAILORS, MERCERS, UPHOLSTERERS, PICTURES, PICTURE-DRAWERS, THE POX, AND DISEASES PROCEEDING FROM UNCLEANNESS. SHE SIGNIFIES ONE MILD OF DISPOSITION; FAIR, BEAUTIFUL, PLEASANT AND MERRY, GIVEN TO MIRTH AND JOLLITY; AND THE AUTHOR OF FRUITFULNESS. SHE FORESHOWS JOY, FRIENDSHIP, MERCY, BOUNTY, LOVE SPORTS, DALLIANCE, DANCING, EMBRACING, KISSING AND SUCH LIKE. BEING HOT AND MOIST, SHE IS THE MISTRESS OF GENERATION, MAKES AN AMIABLE, PLEASANT AND CHEERFUL COUNTENANCE, PRETTILY MIXED WITH RED: SHE GIVES A COMPLETE BODY INCLINING TO TALLNESS, FAIR AND ROUND VISAGED, WITH BEAUTIFUL ROLLING EYES, BROWN OR FLAXEN COLORED HAIR, OF A LOVELY DISPOSITION, GENTLE, BOUNTIFUL, COURTEOUS. BEING ILL PLACED OR DISPOSED, SHE SIGNIFIES WHORES, STRUMPETS, BAWDS, PIMPS, PANDERS, THIEVES, AND SUCH LIKE.

MERCURY

THE AUTHOR OF CRAFT, SUBTLETY, POLICY, DECEIT,
PERJURY, STUDY, HEARING, AND MERCHANDIZING:
HE SIGNIFIES MERCHANTS, CLERKS, SCHOLARS,
SECRETARIES, AMBASSADORS, PAGES, MESSENGERS,
FOES, ORATORS, STATIONERS, CHEATERS, THIEVES,
PETTY LAWYERS, PHILOSOPHERS, MATHEMATICIANS,
ASTROLOGERS. HE SIGNIFIES ONE SWIFT, NIMBLE,
ELOQUENT, INDUSTRIOUS, RATIONAL, A DIVER INTO
ABSTRUSE MYSTERIES, GOOD WITH THE GOOD, BAD
WITH THE BAD, MALE WITH THE MALE, AND FEMALE
WITH THE FEMALE, AN INTERPRETER AND
EXPOUNDER OF THE MYSTERIES OF NATURE; ONE
MUTABLE, CHANGEABLE OR INCONSTANT, LIVELY,
PROMPT, AND OF A READY WIT. HE GIVES A
COMPLEXION NEITHER VERY WHITE, NOR VERY
BLACK, A LONG VISAGE, A HIGH FOREHEAD, SMALL
EYES, BROWN OR ALMOST BLACK, AN EVEN NOSE
AND SOMETHING LONG, THIN BEARD, LONG AND
SLENDER FIGURE, ONE BUSY, SUBTLE, WITTY, SHARP,
AND WARY. BEING ILL PLACED OR DISPOSED, HE
SIGNIFIES THIEVES, CHEATING SOLICITORS, KNAVISH

LAWYERS, KNIGHTS OF THE POST, WITCHES, WIZARDS, DIVINERS, ET CETERA.

LUNA

THE AUTHOR OF POPULAR FAME BOTH GOOD AND EVIL, JOY AND SORROW, MUTABILITY AND INCONSTANCY, AFFECTION, AND DISAFFECTION, MOISTURE, AND EVERY EFFECT WHICH MAY BE SAID TO BE COMMON: SHE SIGNIFIES WATERS, SHIPS, SEAMEN OF ALL SORTS, QUEENS, LADIES, A GOVERNESS, THE COMMON PEOPLE IN GENERAL, NEIGHBORS, MOTHERS, KINDRED, FISHMONGERS, VINTNERS, TAVERNERS, MIDWIVES, NURSES AND TRAVELERS. SHE IS THE TRANSLATOR OF ALL LIGHT FROM ONE PLANET TO ANOTHER, IMPARTING HER LIGHT TO ALL OTHER STARS, AND COMPREHENDING OR RECEIVING THEIR VIRTUES AND POWERS. SHE GIVES COLD AND MOISTURE, FEMININE HONOR AND GLORY, CHASTITY, PITY, MERCY AND THE SUBDUER OF CARNAL AFFECTIONS, TAKING CARE OF ALL STATES AND CONDITIONS OF MEN BOTH BY SEA AND LAND, OVER THE BIRDS OF THE AIR, AND THE BEASTS OF THE FIELD; OVER SERPENTS AT LAND, AND FISHES IN THE WATER, MAKING THINGS TO EBB AND FLOW, ACCORDING TO HER DECREASE OR INCREASE. SHE SHOWS ONE MOVEABLE, BENIGN, INNOCENT, SIMPLE,

CHASTE, AND CURIOUS; GIVES A PALE COUNTENANCE, MIDDLE STATURE, ROUND VISAGE, AND EITHER BLACK, BROWN OR GRAY EYES, ACCORDING AS SHE IS ASPECTED, AND THE SIGN SHE IS IN; TENDER BODY, FLESHY, AND OF A SOFT AND SMOOTH SKIN; ONE THAT IS FACILE OR EASY TO BE ENTREATED, AN AFFECTER OF NEWS AND NEW THINGS, INCONSTANT, ET CETERA. BEING ILL PLACED OR DISPOSED, SHE SIGNIFIES ONE BEETLE BROWED, ILL-NATURED AND A SCOLD.

This being known, understand

First, that the lines take their signification from the mount of that planet from whence they rise.

Secondly, that the place from whence any line rises shows the ground, cause, or original of the things signified by that line; the line or mount to which it points shows the issue to what the thing tends, and what may be the end of the matter significated.

Thirdly, that whether the line signifies good or evil, is it be cut or crossed by any other line, that line so cutting it, will at a certain time not only abate the good, but also take away the evil, if it so signified.

Fourthly, that the nature and quality of that line thus destroying the signification of the former, is known by considering from what place it rises, and to what place it tends.

FIFTHLY, THAT A DOUBLE JUDGMENT ARISES FROM EVERY LINE, BY ACCOUNTING IT, FIRST, FROM THE ONE END; SECONDLY, FROM THE OTHER.

SIXTHLY, THAT LITTLE LINES RISING OUT OF THE SIDES OF ANY OTHER LINE, BOTH AUGMENT THE THINGS SIGNIFIED BY THAT LINE, AND ALSO SIGNIFY NEW MATTER ARISING BY THINGS SIGNIFIED BY THE LINE FROM WHENCE THEY RISE, AND THE PLACE TO WHICH THEY POINT, SHOW TO WHAT THEY TEND.

SEVENTHLY, THAT THE MOUNTS OR LINES ADORNED WITH STARS, OR SMALL LINES NOT ERODED, OR POINTING TO EVIL PLACES, SHOW GREAT GOOD AND HAPPINESS TO THE PERSON, BY THINGS SIGNIFIED BY THE SAME MOUNT OR LINE: AND ON THE CONTRARY, VITIATED WITH CROSSES, SPOTS, OR KNOTS SHOW MUCH EVIL AND PERPLEXITY.

LASTLY, THE BEGINNING OF THE LINES, SHOW IN THE BEGINNING OR FOREPART OF LIFE; THE MIDDLE, IN THE MIDDLE PART OF LIFE; AND THE ENDS OF THEM, THE LATTER PART, OR END OF LIFE, SO THAT IF ANY

EVIL OR GOOD BE SIGNIFIED BY ANY LINE, YOU MUST HINT THE TIME ACCORDING TO THE AFORESAID REASON.

FROM THESE RULES (BEING OBSERVED) YOU MAY ATTAIN TO THE KNOWLEDGE OF THE NATURES, QUALITIES AND DISPOSITIONS OF ALL SORTS OF PEOPLE, THEIR AFFECTIONS AND PASSIONS, ANSWERABLE TO THE VIRTUES AND INFLUENCES OF THE STARS AND PLANETS WHICH THE ANCIENT MATHEMATICIANS AND ASTROLOGERS HAVE BY LONG EXPERIENCE TAKEN NOTICE OF AND OBSERVED, AS DOES SUFFICIENTLY APPEAR BY THEIR WORKS. IT IS TRUE, HERE WE OUGHT TO ENQUIRE INTO THE DENOMINATED TIMES WHEN THE THINGS SIGNIFIED SHOULD COME TO PASS BUT BECAUSE THAT MATTER IS SOMETHING LONG AND ABSTRUSE (BEING MORE FIT TO BE HANDLED IN A PARTICULAR TRACT, WHEREIN ALL ITS CURIOSITIES MAY BE EXAMINED) THIS OUR PRESENT WORK BEING A SUBJECT OF ANOTHER NATURE, AND THESE THINGS NOT ESSENTIAL TO OUR PURPOSE, WE SHALL AT THIS TIME FORBEAR. NOTWITHSTANDING, ALTHOUGH WE HAVE NOT HERE DELINEATED EVERYTHING IN

PARTICULAR, YET WE HAVE LAID (AS IT WERE) THE GROUND AND FOUNDATION OF THE ART, OUT OF WHICH, AS OUT OF A FOUNTAIN, THE INDUSTRIOUS STUDENT MAY AT HIS OWN LEISURE AND PLEASURE, REAR A STATELY FABRIC. BE PLEASED TO VIEW THE SECOND FIGURE OF THE HAND, IN WHICH THE NUMBERS SIGNIFY TEARS: THEREIN YOU MAY PARTLY SEE THE GEOMETRICAL REASON OF THAT MEASURE OF TIME.

Of the Line of Life

I. LINEA VITALIS. THE LINE OF LIFE IS THAT WHICH INCLUDETH THE MOUNT OF THE THUMB.

II. THIS LINE BROAD AND OF A LIVELY COLOR WELL OR LARGELY DRAWN WITHOUT INTERSECTIONS AND POINTS, SHOWS LONG LIFE AND ONE SUBJECT TO FEW DISEASES; BUT SLENDER, SHORT AND BROKEN OR CUT WITH LITTLE CROSS LINES, OF A PALE OR BLACK COLOR, SHOWS SHORT LIFE WITH MANY INFIRMITIES.

III. IF IT MAKES A GOOD ANGLE WITH THE HEPATICA, AND THE ANGLE BE ADORNED WITH PARALLELS OR LITTLE CROSSES, IT SHOWS A GOOD WIT AND A PLEASANT DISPOSITION.

IV. THIS LINEA VITALIS ABOUNDING WITH BRANCHES TOWARDS THE UPPER END, AND THOSE BRANCHES EXTENDING THEMSELVES TOWARDS LINEA HEPATICA FORESHOW RICHES AND HONOR, BUT IF THOSE BRANCHES DESCEND TOWARDS THE RESTRICTA, THEY THREATEN POVERTY, CONTEMPT AND DECEITFUL SERVANTS.

V. IF THIS LINE BE CUT WITH LITTLE LINES LIKE HAIRS, IT SIGNIFIES DISEASES, WHICH IF THEY FALL TOWARDS THE HEPATICA, SHOWS IN THE YOUNGER

YEARS, IN THE MIDDLE OF THE LINE IN THE MIDDLE OF THE AGE, IF TOWARDS THE RESTRICTA, IN THE LATTER YEARS.

VI. IF THIS LINE BE ANYWHERE BROKEN, IT THREATENS GREAT DANGER OF LIFE IN THAT AGE, WHICH THE PLACE OF THE SAID BRANCH BETOKENETH, WHICH YOU MAY FIND OUT WITH A GREAT DEAL OF EXACTNESS, IF YOU DIVIDE THE LINE INTO NINETY EQUAL PARTS, BEGINNING TO NUMBER THEM FROM A TOWARDS B.

VII. IF THE CHARACTER OF SOL (THAT IS TO SAY, ☉) BE FOUND IN THIS LINE, IT SHOWS THE LOSS OF AN EYE, IF TWO SUCH FIGURES, THE LOSS OF BOTH EYES.

VIII. A LINE PASSING THROUGH THIS VITAL TO THE TRIANGLE OF MARS SHOWS WOUNDS AND FEVERS, AND MANY MISFORTUNES IN JOURNEYING.

IX. A LINE PROCEEDING FROM THE VITAL BENEATH THE ANGLE IT MAKES WITH THE HEPATICA TO THE MOUNT OF SATURN, SHOWS AN ENVIOUS MAN, AS ALSO SOME DANGEROUS SATURNIAN DISEASE, AS A CONSUMPTION, ET CETERA, WHICH SHALL FALL IN THOSE YEARS SIGNIFIED BY THAT PART OF THE VITAL LINE WHICH THE SAID LINE TOUCHETH.

X. BUT SUCH A LINE PASSING FROM THE VITAL TO THE RING FINGER, SHOWS HONOR AND WEALTH, AND THAT BY MEANS OF SOME NOBLE WOMAN.

Of the Epatic or Natural Line.

I. The Natural or Liver Line is that which runs from the Life line or Mount of Jupiter through the middle of the palm, terminating generally upon the Mount of Luna.

II. This line straight continued and not cut by other oblique lines, shows a healthy constitution and long life, but short or broken, not reaching beyond the middle of the palm, signifies a short life replete with many diseases.

III. The longer this line is, so much the longer life it signifies, if it be cut at the end thereof, it threatens the end of life with some dangerous disease.

IV. If any breach appears, (yet such a one as seems almost continued) it shows a change of life; if under the middle finger in strength of years, if under the ring-finger, in declining age.

V. If the upper part of it be far distant from the Vital, it shows manifold diseases of the heart, and also a prodigal person.

VI. IF IT BE CROOKED, UNEQUAL, OF VARIOUS COLORS, AND CUT BY OTHER LINES, IT SHOWS AN EVIL HABIT OF THE LIVER AND DISEASES THENCE PROCEEDING, ONE ILL-NATURED AND FOOLISH.

VII. IF STRAIGHT DRAWN AND WELL COLORED, SHOWS WIT, HONOR AND HEALTH.

VIII. IF IT HAS A PARALLEL OR SISTER, IT GIVES INHERITANCES.

IX. IF CONTINUED WITH LITTLE HARD KNOTS, IT SHOWS MURDER ACCORDING TO THE NUMBER OF THOSE KNOTS.

X. IF IT TERMINATES WITH A FORK OR ANGLE TOWARDS THE MOUNT OF LUNA, IT SHOWS A FOOLISH, HYPOCRITICAL, ILL-NATURED PERSON; IF IT TENDS TO THE MENSAL, IT SHOWS A SLANDEROUS AND ENVIOUS PERSON.

XI. WHEN IT CUTS THE VITAL EMINENTLY TO THE MOUNT OF VENUS OR SOROR MARTIS, ESPECIALLY IF THE SAME BE OF A RUDDY COLOR, SHOWS DANGER OF THIEVES AND MANY ILL DISEASES, THREATENING LIFE.

Of the Cephalica or Head-Line

I. The Cephalica ariseth below from the Cardiaca, and is drawn thence to the Epatica, thereby making a triangular figure.

II. Making such a perfect figure, and it having a lively color, without intersection, declares one of great prudence, and a person of no vulgar wit or fortune.

III. So much the more perfect the triangle, much the more fortunate, and it shows a man very wise, temperate and courageous.

IV. If the triangle be obtuse, it shows an evil nature, clownish and rude; if there be no triangle, it is still worse, and shows the person to be foolish, a liar and prodigal, and generally one of a short life.

V. The higher angle being right, or not very acute, shows a generous man, but if it be very acute, or if it touch the Line of Life under the mount of the middle finger, it declares a miserable, hard and covetous wretch, it also foreshows a consumption.

VI. The left angle being made upon the Epatica in the ferient (being a right angle) shows a profound understanding.

VII. The Cephalica casting unequal and irregular clefts to Mons Luna, thereby constituting strange characters, shows a dull head, and danger by the sea in men: but in women, discontents, miscarriages and the like.

VIII. But casting equal lines, it presages the contrary in both sexes: to wit, in men wisdom, and success at sea, and in women, contentment and happy childbearing.

IX. If the Cephalica make a cleft or apparent star, upward to the Cavea Martis, it shows boldness, and magnanimity of mind: but if it let the same fall downward, it manifests deceit and cowardice.

X. The Cephalica joined to the Restricta, by a remarkable concourse, shows a happy and joyful old age.

XI. But if it be drawn upwards, (in form like a fork.) towards the place of Fortune, it shows

MUCH SUBTLETY AND CRAFT IN THE MANAGEMENT
OF AFFAIRS.

XII. IF IN THIS FORK, THE CHARACTER OF ⊕ SORS BE
FOUND, IT SHOWS RICHES AND HONOR, BY THE
MAN'S OWN INDUSTRY.

Of the Mensal Line, or Line of Fortune.

I. The Mensal or Line of Fortune (called also Linea Thoralis) takes its original from under the Mount of Mercury, and extends itself towards the Mount of Jupiter.

II. This line if it be long enough and without incisures shows strength of body, and constancy of mind; the contrary if it be short, crooked or cut.

III. If it terminates under the Mount of Saturn, it shows a foolish, idle and deceitful person.

IV. If in this line be found certain pricks or points, it shows a lecherous person.

V. If the Epatica be wanting; and the Mensal be annexed to the Vital, it foreshows either beheading, hanging or other untimely death.

VI. If from the Mensal, a line ascends to the space between the Mounts of Jupiter and Saturn, another to the space between the Mounts of Saturn and Sol; and a third to the space between the Mounts of Sol and

MERCURY, IT SIGNIFIES AN ENVIOUS, TURBULENT AND CONTENTIOUS PERSON.

VII. A LITTLE LINE ONLY THUS DRAWN TO THE SPACE BETWEEN THE MONS SATURNI AND SOLIS, SHOWS LABOR AND SORROW.

VIII. IF ANNEXED TO THE EPATICA, MAKING THEREWITH AN ACUTE ANGLE, THE SAME.

IX. THE MENSAL PROJECTING SMALL BRANCHES TO THE MONS JOVIS, SHOWS HONOR AND GLORY.

X. BUT IF IT BE NAKED OR SINGLE, IT SHOWS POVERTY AND DISTRESS.

XI. IF IT CUTS THE MOUNT OF JUPITER, IT SHOWS A COVETOUS MIND, AND GREAT PRIDE.

XII. IF IT SEND A BRANCH BETWEEN THE MONS JOVIS AND SATURNI, IT SHOWS IN A MAN, A WOUND IN HIS HEAD; BUT IN A WOMAN, MISCARRIAGE OR DANGER CHILDBEARING.

XIII. CONFUSED LITTLE LINES IN THE MENSAL, SHOW SICKNESS AND DISEASES; IF UNDER THE MONS SATURNI, IN YOUTH; IF UNDER THE MONS SOLIS, IN THE MIDDLE AGE; UNDER THE MONS MERCURIS, IN OLD AGE.

XIV. LASTLY, IF THERE BE NO MENSAL AT ALL, IT SHOWS ONE FAITHLESS, BASE, INCONSTANT AND MALICIOUS.

Of the Restricta, or Cauda Draconis.

I. The Restricta is that line which divides the hand from the arm, either by a single, double or triple anscursion; thereby determining subject of art; which by some is called the Discriminal Line.

II. If the Restricta be double or triple, and extended in a right and continued tract, it shows a healthful constitution of body, and long life.

III. That line which is nearest the hand continued without incisure, and of a good color, shows riches.

IV. But if it be pale or crooked or cut in the middle, it shows weakness of body and poverty.

V. A line drawn from the Restricta to Mon Luna, shows poverty, imprisonment and private enemies.

VI. If that line be crooked, it doubles all the evil, and shows a perpetual slavery or misery.

VII. But such a line being clear and straight, and extended to the Mons Lunae, shows

MANY JOURNEYS AND PEREGRINATIONS BOTH BY SEA AND LAND.

VIII. IF IT EXTEND TO THE MONS JOVIS, IT FORESHOWS ESTIMATION AND ECCLESIASTIC DIGNITY, BUT THAT THE MAN SHALL LIVE IN A STRANGE COUNTRY.

IX. IF TO THE EPATICA, IT SHOW HONESTY, TRUTH AND SINCERITY, AND ONE OF A HEALTHFUL AND LONG LIFE.

X. IF TO THE MONS SOLIS A GREAT AND CERTAIN GOOD, AND GIVES HONOR AND COMMAND IN THE COMMONWEALTH.

XI. AND SO FROM THE SAME REASON, PASSING TO THE MONS MERCURII, IT SHOWS A LEARNED AND INGENIOUS SOUL; BUT IF IT REACH NOT THAT MOUNT, BUT IS BROKEN ABOUT THE MIDDLE, IT SHOWS A LYING, PRATING, IDLE PERSON.

XII. IF IT ASCENDS DIRECTLY TO THE MONS SATURNI, IT SHOWS AN INHERITANCE IN LAND: BUT IF IT BE CROOKED, IT SHOWS A COVETOUS PERSON, AND ONE OF A VERY ILL NATURE.

XIII. A LINE RUNNING FROM THE RESTRICTA, THROUGH THE MONS VENERIS, SHOWS POVERTY,

ADVERSITY AND WANT, AND THAT BY MEANS OF SOME WOMEN OR WOMANKIND.

XIV. A CROSS OR STAR UPON THE RESTRICTA, SHOWS A HAPPY AND LONG LIFE.

XV. ONE OR MORE STARS UPON THE RESTRICTA BY THE MONS VENERIS, IN WOMEN, SHOWS LEWDNESS, DISHONOR AND INFAMY.

Of the Saturnia, or Line of Saturn.

I. This line is that which ascends from The Restricta, through the middle of the Vola, to the Mons Saturni, which line if it be cut or parted, is called Via Combusta.

II. This being full, and extended to the Mons Saturni, shows a man of profound cogitations, of great wisdom, and an admirable counselor in all great actions.

III. If it be combust, it is an evil sign, foreshowing many misfortunes, and poverty in one part of life.

IV. A line drawn from the Vital through the Epatica, to the Mons Saturni, making an angle with the Linea Saturnia, foreshows imprisonment, and captivity, and many misfortunes.

V. The Saturnia bending backwards in Cavea Martis towards the Ferient, the same.

VI. This line filled with unusual and inauspicious characters shows unhappiness and disasters.

VII. A GROSS LINE RUNNING FROM THE INTERVAL OF
THE MONS JOVIS TO THE MENSAL, AND BREAKING
OR CUTTING OF IT, SHOWS DISEASES OR WOUNDS IN
THE BELLY OR PARTS ADJACENT

Of the Mount of Jupiter.

I. The Mount of Jupiter is the tuberculum under the forefinger.

II. If upon the Mount of Jupiter there be a star or a double cross it foreshows riches, prosperity, and happiness, one born to noble and glorious actions, one honest, affable, courteous, and renowned, a generous foul indeed, and faithful in all their undertakings.

III. The same, if this Mount is adorned with a parallel line, or a line sweetly drawn, between it and the Vital; it shows great dignities, and estimation with great men.

IV. But if this Mount be vitiated, with a character like a half gridiron, it shows unhappiness, calamities, poverty, disgrace and deposition from honors and dignities; losses by women-kind, and diseases in the heart and lungs.

V. The same if a line cutting this Mount, tends to the Mount or the Line of Saturn; this also threatens and apoplexy.

VI. Lastly, a cross, but especially a clear red star on this mount, is a signal and sure demonstration of a splendid life, replete with honor and glory, riches and an eternal name.

Of the Cavea of Mars, and the Via Martis

I. The Cavea Martis is the hollow in the middle of the palm, commonly called the Triangle of Mars, made of the three principal lines, to wit, the Cardiaca, Cephalica and Epatica.

II. The Via or Linea Martis (called also the Vital Sister and Soror Martis) is a parallel to the line of Life on the Mons Veneris.

III. Mars is fortunate, so often as the Soror Martis appears red, clear and sweetly drawn, and when either stars or crosses are found in his Cavea, or triangle; and thereby is signified courage, boldness, magnanimity, fortitude and strength: the man is imperious, strong and a great eater.

IV. But if the triangle be infortunated by evil lines from the Mons Veneris or Lunae, the person is litigious, scornful, proud, disdainful, deceitful, and wicked: a Thief, a Lecher, Robber, Murderer, and shall have a life wholly filled with unhappiness.

V. The character of ♄ Saturn in the triangle, shows a danger of falling from some high place.

VI. A crooked line ascending from the triangle to the Mons Saturni, shows imprisonment.

VII. A line from the said triangle towards the Restricta, terminating under the Mons Lunae, shows many peregrinations, journeys and travels.

VIII. The Soror Martis augments all the good signified by the Cardiaca or Line of Life, but particularly it promises success in war and the love of women.

Of the Mount of the Sun, and Via Solis.

I. The Mount of the Sun is the tuberculum under the ring finger.

II. The Via Solis is a right line running down from the Mount of Sol, to the Triangle of Mars.

III. A star or stars upon the Mons Solis, shows one faithful and ingenious, and that he shall attain to great honor, glory and dignity, be honored of Kings, Princes and great men; one of a great and magnanimous spirit, wise, just and religious.

IV. But a perpendicular thereon cut or crossed with a line from the Mons Saturni, shows pride, and arrogancy, a boaster, a poor base spirit, and one that shall fall into irrecoverable miseries.

V. The Via Solis clear, and not broken, or cut by any ill line, shows honor in the commonwealth and the favors of Kings and great Princes.

VI. But it being cut or confused, or hurt by any line from either the Mount of line of

SATURN, IT SHOWS THE CONTRARY: POVERTY AND
THE HATRED OF GREAT MEN.

Of the Mount of Venus, and the Cingulum Veneris.

I. The Mount of Venus is the tuberculum of the thumb.

II. The Cingulum Veneris, or girdle of Venus, is a piece or segment of a circle drawn from the interval or space between the Mons Jovis and Saturni, to the interval or space between the Mons Solis and Mercurii.

III. A clear star, or furrows that be fed and transversely parallel upon the Mons Veneris, and is much elevated, shows one merry, cheerful and amorous; it shows also one faithful, just and entire, one with whom an incorrupted tie of friendship (being once made) is durable forever: it also signifies great fortune or estate and substance by a sweetheart or lover.

IV. But this Mount infortunated by evil lines, or lines from evil places, and irregular figures shows a lecherous person, an adulterer, a poor, base, sordid wretch, who shall spend his substance on whores.

V. The character of the △ trine aspect on this Mount, shows a great fortune by marriage.

VI. The Mount of Venus void of lines and incisures, shows a rude, effeminate and foolish person, and one ridiculous, and unfortunate in wedlock.

VII. The Cingulum Veneris, or girdle of Venus, shows intemperance and lust in both sexes, a base and bestial life; a filthy sodomite, who abuses himself with beasts.

VIII. If it be broken or disaffected, it shows infamy and disgrace by lust and lechery.

Of the Mount of Mercury

I. THE MOUNT OF MERCURY IS THE TUBERCULUM UNDER THE LITTLE FINGER.

II. THIS MOUNT, HAPPY AND FORTUNATE WITH A STAR, OR PARALLEL CROSSES, OR THE CHARACTER OF THE Δ TRINE ASPECT, SHOWS WIT AND INGENUITY, AND MAKES THE PERSON A GREAT ORATOR, GIVES HIM SUBSTANCE BY ARTS AND SCIENCES, AND THE UNDERSTANDING OF SECRET MYSTERIES IN ALCHEMY, MUSIC, PAINTING , ASTROLOGY AND PHILOLOGY, AND RAISES THE PERSON TO DIGNITY BY MEANS OF HIS OWN WIT, PRUDENCE AND INDUSTRY.

III. BUT THIS MOUNT AFFLICTED, OR WITHOUT LINES, OR HURT BY A LINE FROM THE MOUNT OF SATURN, (CUTTING THE MOUNT OF SOL) OR FROM THE TRIANGLE OF MARS, SHOWS A POOR, LOW AND DULL WIT, A PERSON OF NO AUDACITY OR COURAGE, A MERE COWARD, A LIAR, PRATTLER, THIEF, CHEAT, TRAITOR, AND ONE FAITHLESS, AND SOMETIMES MELANCHOLY, MAD OR FRANTIC.

IV. THESE JUDGMENTS ARE THE MORE FIRM WHERE THE LINES AND SIGNATURES ARE FAIR, FIRM AND

CLEAR: BUT IF THEY BE DULL OR OBSCURE, THESE JUDGMENTS ARE MORE DUBIOUS AND INTRICATE.

V. A LINE FROM THE MONS LUNAE TO THE MONS MERCURII NOT CUT OR BROKEN, SHOWS A MAN EMINENT AND FAMOUS IN HIS TRADE OR PROFESSION (AMONG THE COMMON PEOPLE) LET IT BE WHAT IT WILL.

Of the Mons Lunae, and the Via Lactea

I. The Mons Lunae (called also *Feriens à Feriendo*, the smiting part) is the mount comprehended under the Tuberculum of Mercury, between the Mensal and Restricta.

II. The Via Lactea or Milky Way, is the line running upwards from the Restricta through the Feriens or Mons Lunae.

III. The Mons Lunae filled with happy characters (as we have before hinted) shows one honest, just and honorable, and makes a man famous through a kingdom, gives him the praise of the common people, and the acquaintance of great and noble ladies; and makes him happy in navigation.

IV. But being infortunated by evil characters, or a trapezia, or evil lines from the Triangle of Mars, or lines broken, or cut with oblique angles, it shows one of a various, poor and inconstant life, a beggar, a person envied by almost all people, one wicked, treacherous and deceitful, a person subject to travel, captivity or banishment.

V. If the good lines on the ferient be fair and comely, they premonstrate so much the more happiness, and in women fruitfulness; but the evil lines pale, so much the more evil.

VI. The Via Lactea or Milky Way, well-proportioned and continued, shows fortunate journeys, both by sea and land, great wit, and the love and favor of womankind, chiefly of ladies and great women.

VII. But if this line be cut or crooked, it shows unhappiness, and a poor and low estate.

VIII. If it be whole and extended to the little finger, it shows a great good beyond expectation.

Of the Mensa, or Table

I. The Mensa is the interval or space betwixt the Mensal and Epatica, the which is given or at tribute to Fortune, from whence the Table is called the place of Fortune.

II. The Mensa being large and broad, and replete with good figures, shows riches and treasure, one of a liberal, magnanimous spirit, and of long life.

III. But small and narrow, shows poverty or a slender and mean fortune, a niggard, a coward, a pitiful, poor, fearful and mean soul.

IV. A little circle in the Mensa shows a great wit, and a profound person in arts and sciences.

V. The Mensa terminating in an angle under Mons Jovis by the concourse of the Mensal and Cardiac or Vital line shows falsehood and treachery, and one of short life.

VI. A cross or star, within it, clear and of good proportion, especially under the Mount of Sol, shows honor and dignity, by means of

GREAT AND NOBLE MEN, AND INCREASE OF NOBLEMEN: IF IT BE THE CHARACTER OF ♃ JUPITER, IT SHOWS ECCLESIASTICAL PREFERMENT.

VII. THE SAME CROSS OR STAR, BEING DOUBLED OR TRIPLED WONDERFULLY INCREASETH THE AFORESAID GOOD FORTUNE; BUT CUT OR CONFUSED BY OTHER LITTLE LINES, THE SAID GOOD IS MUCH DIVERTED, AND ANXIETIES AND TROUBLES THREATENED.

VIII. GOOD AND EQUAL LINES IN THE MENSA, SHOW GOOD FORTUNE; EVIL AND DISTORTED OR CROOKED, THE CONTRARY.

IX. A CROSS OR STAR IN THE MENSA OVER MONS LUNAE SHOWS FORTUNACY IN TRAVELLING.

X. IF THERE BE NO MENSA, IT SHOWS A CLOUDY AND OBSCURE LIFE AND FORTUNE.

Of the Thumb and Fingers.

I. A line surrounding the Pollex or thumb in the middle joint, shows the person shall be hanged.

II. A line passing from the upper joint of the Pollex to the Cardiaca, shows a violent death, or danger by means of some married woman.

III. Overthwart lines, clear and long underneath the nail and joint of the thumb, show riches and honor.

IV. Equal furrows drawn under the lower joint thereof, show riches and inheritances.

V. The first and second joint free from incisures, show a slothful and idle person.

VI. Overthwart lines in the uppermost joint of the index or forefinger, show inheritances; but such in the middle joint, show a subtle person.

VII. Right lines running between those joints in the index, show (in women) a plentiful issue; (in men) a nimble tongue.

VIII. If they be in the first joint near Mons Jovis, they show a pleasant and courteous disposition; and a man of a generous soul.

IX. But a woman who hath a star in the same place, is lascivious and whorish.

X. Little gridirons in the joints of the Medius or middle finger: an unfortunate and melancholy person; but equal and parallel lines show fortune by dealing in metals.

XI. A star there, shows a violent death by drowning or witchcraft, or the like.

XII. A gross line rising from the Mons Saturni, through the whole finger to the end thereof, shows a mere fool or mad person.

XIII. And as in the Mounts, good or evil characters are omens of good or evil fortunes; so also on the fingers they signify the same.

XXIX. The first joint near the Mount shows the first age: the second joint, middle age: and the last joint, old age; but it is our opinion, that the directions of the principal significators in every geniture, more properly

DEMONSTRATE THE TIMES IN WHICH THE GOOD OR EVIL SIGNIFIED BY THOSE MARKS OR LINES MAY PROBABLY HAPPEN.

THE GOOD AND EVIL LINES, MARKS OR CHARACTERS

I. THE GOOD LINES, MARKS OR CHARACTERS ARE PARALLELS, AS = OR ‖ DOUBLE OR TRIPLE, AND THE LIKE, CROSSES AS + OR X : DOUBLE CROSSES AND THE LIKE; STARS AS THE SEXTILE ASPECT * OR THE LIKE: LADDERS-STEPS AND QUADRANGLES AS □ : THE TRINE ASPECT; AS △ : ANGLES AS THE RIGHT OR ACUTE, OR A MULT-ANGLE, &C. THE CHARACTERS OF JUPITER AND VENUS, AS ♃♀ , AND OTHER THE LIKE AKIN TO THESE.

II. THE UNFORTUNATE AND EVIL CHARACTERS ARE DEFORMED, IRREGULAR AND UNCOUTH FIGURES, BROKEN LINES, CROOKED LINES, GRIDIRONS, THE CHARACTERS OF ♄ SATURN AND ♂ MARS: THE OPPOSITION 8 : IRREGULAR CIRCLES, OBTUSE ANGLES AND SUCH LIKE.

III. LASTLY, AS, THE QUANTITY OF LINES CONSIDERED IN THEIR LENGTH AND DEPTH; THEIR QUALITY, IN THEIR SHAPE AND COMPLEXION; THEIR ACTION, IN TOUCHING OR CUTTING OTHER LINES; THEIR PASSION, IN BEING TOUCHED OR CUT OF OTHERS;

AND THEIR PLACE IN WHICH THEY ARE POSITED OR LOCATED, OUGHT TO BE OBSERVED; SO ALSO THEIR TIME OF APPEARING OR DISAPPEARING, OUGHT NOT TO PASS OUR COGNIZANCE.

IV. FOR IT IS MOST CERTAIN THAT SOME LINES ARE PROLONGED TO CERTAIN YEARS OF OUR AGE, OTHERSOME SHORTENED; SOMETIMES THEY WAX PALE, SOMETIMES GROW RED; SOME OF ONE SHAPE QUITE VANISH, WHILE OTHERS OF ANOTHER SHAPE RISE: NOW THE CAUSE WITHOUT DOUBT IS THE VARIOUS PROGRESSIONS OF THE APHETICAL PLACES IN THE GENITURE, TO THEIR VARIOUS AND CONTINGENT PROMISORS, TO THE INFLUENCE OF WHICH, THE WHOLE MAN ITSELF IS SUBJUGATED; AND THEREFORE IT BEHOOVES THE INDUSTRIOUS AND STUDIOUS ARTIST, NOT TO DETERMINE ALL THINGS AT FIRST SIGHT, FOR NO MAN CAN ATTAIN THE KNOWLEDGE OF ALL PARTICULARS AT ONE INSPECTION; BUT YEARLY TO MAKE NEW OBSERVATIONS, AS THE PERSON INCREASES IN AGE.

V. MOREOVER IT IS TO BE OBSERVED, THAT THESE JUDGMENTS BE NOT DELIVERED SIMPLY ALONE, BUT BY BEING COMPARED WITH THE RULES DELIVERED IN THE FIRST PART OF THE LESSON, FROM WHENCE

MANY OTHER PROGNOSTICS MORE THAN WHAT WE HAVE HERE MENTIONED WILL ARISE, TO THE INFINITE PLEASURE OF THE ARTIST, AND SATISFACTION OF THE CURIOUS INQUISITOR.

Certain Chiromantical Aphorisms

I. Incisures and crosses upon the Mount of Saturn show some light adversities and diseases.

II. Two, three, or more little lines on the first joint of the little finger, shows the dominion of Mercury, and an acute wit.

III. The Mons Veneris notably furrowed, shows wantonness, and one that shall obtain many loves.

IV. A large and broad Mensa, shows a free and liberal soul: and if it be adorned with good figures, an accumulation of much treasures and riches.

V. The Saturnia only touching the Epatica shows one ingenious, and of long life.

VI. Mons Jovis well adorned with good figures, demonstrates the height of honor.

VII. A cross near or upon the Ferient, shows auspicious and profitable journeys, and honorable.

VIII. A cross in the Mensa under the Annular shows honor, glory and treasure: but if any

OF ITS LINES BE CUT BY THE EPATICA, IT SHOWS LOSS OF SUBSTANCE IN OLD AGE.

IX. TWO, THREE, OR MORE PARALLEL LINES UPON THE FERIENT, SHOWS MANY PROFITABLE AND PLEASANT JOURNEYS.

X. TWO OR THREE PARALLEL LINES UPON THE MONS MERCURII, INCLINES TO ALL MANNER OF ARTS AND SCIENCES, AND GIVES A PROFOUND WIT.

XI. THE VIA SOLIS, NOT HURT, SHOWS HONORS, BUT IF IT BE CUT OR TOUCHED BY OTHER LINES, SOME IMPEDIMENT THEREIN: IF THE OBSTRUCTIVE LINE ARISES FROM THE MONS MERCURII, BY SOME MERCURIAL MAN OR THING OR THE LIKE: IF FROM THE MONS LUNAE, FROM SOME WOMANKIND, THE COMMON PEOPLE, OR SOME VULGAR BUSINESS; IF FROM THE MONS SATURNI, FROM SOME OLD MAN OR MEN, SOME WORN OUT PRIEST OR PROPHET, OR INFORMER, OR OTHER SATURNIAN MATTER: THE LIKE JUDGE OF IT ARISES FROM OTHER PARTS.

XII. PARALLEL LINES UPON THE MONS SATURNI FALLING UPON, AND CUTTING THE MENSAL LINE, SHOWS SICKNESS, POVERTY, AND WANT IN OLD AGE.

XIII. The cutting of the Vital, shows diseases about those years, which the parts of the line cut signify.

XIV. If the line cutting the Vital, comes from the Triangle of Mars, it shows wounds, or a burning fever, or the French Pox: If it comes from the Saturnia, it shows melancholy, a consumption, or a fall.

XV. The Soror Martis very conspicuous and eminent, shows boldness and courage, and one that will be fortunate and formidable in war.

XVI. An except good Cephalica, shows an incomparable ingenuity.

XVII. A cross upon the Mons Lunae declares fruitfulness and many children; as also safe delivery in child bearing.

XVIII. The Saturnia rising obliquely from the Restricta, to the Mons Saturni, shows labor and sorrow; and one of a covetous disposition.

XIX. A line arising from the middle of the hand, cutting the Epatica, and ascending to the extremity of the Mensal, under the Mons

MERCURII, SHOWS IN THE DECLINING AGE AN
UNFAITHFUL FRIEND OR FRIENDS, FROM WHOM
SHALL COME LOSS AND DETRIMENT.

XX. CROSS OR STAR NEAR OR UPON THE EPATICA,
SHOWS SOME IMMINENT GOOD.

XXI. AS THE MONS SATURNI AFFLICTED, FORESHOWS
DISEASES; SO THOSE DISEASES ARE CHIEFLY THE GOUT
OR A CONSUMPTION: IF THE LINE AFFLICTING THE
MONS SATURNI, ARISES FROM THE TRIANGLE OF
MARS, IT DECLARES EITHER AN HECTIC OR THE
STONE.

XXII. THE CINGULUM VENERIS, GENERALLY SHOWS
INTEMPERANCES BUT IF IT BE INTERSECTED OR CUT,
IT IS A POSITIVE SIGN OF SENSUALITY AND
LASCIVIOUSNESS; AND THAT THE PERSON SHALL
SUFFER IN REPUTATION AND GOOD NAME, AND NOT
WITHOUT CAUSE: AND OFTENTIMES FORESHOWS
WANT IF ISSUE.

XXIII. THE TRIANGLE OF MARS BEING PERFECT; THE
SATURNIA EXTENDED ONLY TO THE TOUCHING OF
THE EPATICA; THE CEPHALICA CONTINUED TO THE
MONS MERCURII, AND THE VIA LACTEA VERY FAIR,
ARE FIRM ARGUMENTS OF ONE EXCEEDING
FORTUNATE.

XXIV. Parallel lines drawn from the Mounts of Saturn and Sol, to the Mons Lunae, shows increase of fortune and substance in foreign countries, and in traveling; as also from some eminent lady or ladies, womankind, the common people, and things lunar.

XXV. The Mensal cutting the Mons Jovis shows one passionate, and full of wrath: if the same be cut under the Mons Saturni, by a short and thick line, it shows some grievous distemper in the bowels and lower part of the belly.

XXVI. The Via Lactea, arising from the Restricta and Vital shows an old age full of tranquility and so much the more, if the end thereof upon the Mons Lunae be adorned with a cross or star, or parallel line.

XXVII. The Epatica inclined towards the Restricta (thereby making a narrow triangle) makes one not over wise, yet covetous.

XXVIII. A line coming from the Vital into the Triangulum Martis making a cross with the Saturni shows wounds and danger of life by

THIEVES AND SUCH LIKE: THE SAME CROSS SHOWS FEVERS ALSO.

XXIX. THE SAME IS SIGNIFIED IF THE MENSAL BE CONJOINED WITH THE EPATICA BY ANY INTERVENING LINE.

XXX. A CROSS OR STAR ON THE UPPER PART OF THE MONS VENERIS SHOWS UNLAWFUL LOVES AND A LECHER; THIS IS THE MORE CONFIRMED IF THE SAID MOUNT BE WELL ADORNED WITH FURROWS.

XXXI. A SISTER JOINED UNTO THE SATURNIA, CONFIRMS ITS SIGNIFICATIONS DOUBLE.

XXXII. THE CEPHALICA EXTENDED EVEN TO THE MONS MERCURII SHOWS ELOQUENCE, A READY WIT, AND MUCH INGENUITY.

XXXIII. IF THE VIA SOLIS APPEARS NOT IN THE HAND, THE FAVORS OF PRINCES AND GREAT MEN WILL NOT BE EASILY ATTAINED.

XXXIV. A LINE RUNNING FROM THE VITAL TO THE MONS JOVIS (BUT ESPECIALLY PASSING THROUGH THE VITAL) SHOWS GREATNESS AND HONOR, AND THAT SOMETIMES TO COME BY WOMANKIND, OR BY MARRIAGE.

XXXV. The Mensal projecting little branches towards the Ferient under the Tuberculum Mercurii presages poverty.

XXXVI. A line falling from the intervals of the Mons Saturni and Jovis threatens a dangerous wound, in the lower part of the belly.

XXXVII. The Vital dissected by a line from the Mons Saturni, shows a dangerous Saturnian disease: from the Mons Jovis, a disease of his nature: from the Mons Solis, a solar disease: from the Mons Mecurii one whimsical, or afflicted with a Mercurial distemper: from the Triangulum Martis a Martial disease, as some wound or burning fever: from the Mons Luna, madness, dropsy, or some other Lunar disaffection.

XXXVIII. The Mensal or Line of Fortune, cut by a line from the Mons Jovis, shows loss or damages by things or persons Jovial: by a line from the Mons Saturni or Linea Saturnia by things or persons Saturnine: by a line from the Mons Mercurii, by scriveners, pettifoggers, and things or persons Mercurial.

XXXIX. A line running from the Mons Saturni to the Mons Luna, parallel to the Vital, shows wonderful preferment and dignities, and a person formidable but not without great envy.

XL. The Soror Martis, running through the Vital to the Mons Jovis, shows the ☌ or other aspect of ♃ and ♂ in the geniture.

XLI. The Restricta not broken or cut, but continued, and of a good color, argues riches, and a healthful constitution of body.

XLII. The Cephalica having a Sister, confirms the significations thereof, let them be what they will: and if the said Sister reaches to the Epatica, it shows one crafty and subtle, and excellent in managing of affairs.

XLIII. Good lines upon the Mons Solis being cut shows honors; but full of troubles.

XLIV. Parallel incisures on the Mons Lunae, tending to the place of Mars, show long journeys.

XLV. The Epatica extremely produced, argues a very long life.

XLVI. A cross in the utmost part of the Mensa near the Ferient, and another in the Cephalica near the Restricta denotes a plentiful life in old age, and many successful journeys.

XLVII. A cross in the Cavea Martis shows an inclination to arms and martial discipline, and sometimes wounds.

XLVIII. The Saturnia whole, and extended through the Epatica and Mensal, shows a happy success and event of actions, and one of profound cogitations.

XLIX. A line coming from the Mons Jovis to the Mons Veneris (not cut by any evil line) presages a great fortune by marriage.

L. A cross just above the Restricta between the Mons Veneris and the Mons Lunae, shows tranquility and happiness in old age.

LI. The Mensal full of branches (almost like a herringbone) and they pointing towards the Mons Jovis, eminently declare an increase of riches.

LII. The character of ♃ Jupiter in the Mensa under Mons Solis, shows preferment Ecclesiastical.

LIII. Parallel lines in Triangulum Martis, pointing towards the Ferient, argue felicity and much good.

LIV. A cross or star, upon the end of the Saturni near the Restricta, shows uprightness of mind, one courteous and peaceable, and obtaining a happy and pleasant old age.

LV. A line from the Vital, falling upon, and cutting the Epatica, shows shortness of life, and an hot liver.

LVI. The Saturnia falling from the Mons Saturni to the Mons Luna, shows adversities and secret enemies, and if it then turns back like a hook towards the Mons Mercurii, it signifies captivity or imprisonment.

LVII. The Cingulum Veneris cut by lines from the Mons Saturni or Mons Solis, denotes diseases, and hurts by lasciviousness.

LVIII. The Via Solis cut by the Cingulum Veneris, brings a stain upon the honor by some womankind.

LIX. Parallel lines from the Mons Veneris to the Mons Mercurii, shows a conjunction or other aspect of Venus and Mercury in the geniture, and signify great eloquence.

LX. A crooked line falling from the Mons Saturni into the Cavea Martis, threatens a fall from a high place, or drowning, and this so much the more imminently as the line is more crooked.

12828345R00115

Printed in Great Britain
by Amazon.co.uk, Ltd.,
Marston Gate.